# Reservations and Ticketing
## with
# SABRE

## Dennis L. Foster

**MUNDUS**

# Table of Contents

# Introduction

## Objectives

*After completing this unit, you should be able to do the following:*

1. Identify the basic components of a computer reservation system.
2. Sign in and sign out.
3. Encode and decode airlines, cities, aircraft equipment, and countries.

The computer is one of the most influential inventions of the century-indeed, of all time. Almost every human endeavor has benefited in one way or another from the rapid spread of computers. Yet it was not long ago that computers were rare and their role in the affairs of humanity was minor. Sixty years ago, there were virtually no computers anywhere in the world. In 1950, there were about 250 computers. Today, more than 300 million computers are in use throughout the world.

Until the late 1960s, only the largest companies and government agencies could afford computers. The development of Large Scale Integration (LSI) allowed thousands of electrical circuits to be placed on a small slice of silicon, called a microprocessor. In 1982, IBM Corporation introduced the personal computer, or "PC." Today, the term PC is commonly used in a general sense to refer to any computer which uses a microprocessor.

## Global Distribution Systems

A computer reservation system (CRS) is based on a large central computer, or mainframe, serving many sites, such as travel agencies and airport offices. A CRS that is distributed worldwide may also be referred to as a global distribution system (GDS). A small travel office may have as few as two terminals, whereas a busy airline reservation center may have more than 100 terminals.

The SABRE central computer is located in Tulsa, Oklahoma in the United States, and serves users in both hemispheres. The part of the mainframe that processes data is called the central processing unit, or CPU. Flight information, airfares, and reservation data are stored in the mainframe's storage unit.

A terminal is often referred to as a CRT (cathode ray tube), the type of television tube that is used for the display of information. Another abbreviation for a computer terminal is VDT (video display terminal). PCs are commonly used in travel agencies to communicate with computer reservation systems.

## Computers and The Tourism Industry

Nowhere has the impact of computer technology been more profound than in the tourism industry. Over the last 30 years, the computer has become an essential tool of airlines, hotel chains, car rental companies, and travel agencies.

SABRE provides users with access to airline flight schedules, fare information, hotel rates, car rentals, and other essential travel data. When a reservation is booked by a travel agency, the information is stored by the system and transmitted to the vendor. In many cases, SABRE can provide direct access to the airline's reservation system. SABRE provides availability and fare displays for more than 500 participating passenger carriers, 30 car rental companies, and most hotel chains and cruise lines.

**Sign In/Sign Out**

Before the system can be used to access airline fares or book passenger reservations, the travel agent must first "sign in" at the CRT. The sign-in procedure identifies the agent and the work area in which he or she will be working.

The work area is a temporary storage area assigned to each terminal. In the work area, the agent assembles information such as the traveler's name, contact telephone numbers, and the desired ticketing date. In general, the information may be entered in any order. Together, this collection of data is referred to as a passenger name record, or PNR. When the data is complete, the agent inputs the entry to end the transaction. This action sends the record to the central computer for permanent storage. The work area is then cleared so that another PNR can be assembled.

**Sign-In**

The sign-in entry is used to identify the agent and gain access to the computer. To sign in to SABRE, the agent inputs the following entry:

SI<Work Area><Sign-In Code>

**Example:**
SI*37634

This example will sign in to all work areas. The following will sign in to a specific work area:

SIA*01762

This entry will sign in only to area A.

**Sign Out**

Before leaving the terminal for an extended time, and at the conclusion of each business day, the agent is instructed to sign out, as follows:

SO*

This entry is used to sign out of all work areas. The following entry will sign out of a specific work area:

SOA

If the terminal is not used for one hour, the agent is signed out automatically.

# Encoding and Decoding

The encoding function is used to convert a name to a code, whereas the decoding function is used to convert a code to a name.

**City and Airport Codes**

Cities and airports are indicated by three-letter codes. For example, Paris has the city code PAR, and Chicago has the code CHI. If a city has multiple airports, each airport has a different code. For example, CDG is the code for Paris-Charles de Gaulle, and ORY is the code for Paris-Orly. The city code NYC refers to all New York City airports, whereas JFK refers specifically to John F. Kennedy International and LGA refers to LaGuardia.

City and airport codes are designated by the International Standards Organization (ISO) based in Geneva, Switzerland. All computer reservation systems recognize these codes.

**Encoding a City or Airport**

The entry code W/-CC is used to encode a city, as follows:

W/-CC<City or airport>

**Example**
W/-CCLUXOR

This example will display the city code for Luxor. The entry code W/-AP is used to encode an airport, as follows:

W/-APHEATHROW

This entry will display the airport code for Heathrow.

**Decoding a City or Airport**

The entry code W/* is used to decode either a city code or an airport code, as follows:

W/*<City or airport code>

**Example**
W/*FCO

**Carrier Codes**

Passenger carriers are referred to by two-letter and three-letter carrier codes. For example, the carrier code for Air France is AF, and the code for Lufthansa is LH. The International Air Transport Association (IATA), which represents more than 200 of the world's principal airlines, assigns carrier codes. IATA has also assigned a three-digit airline code to each carrier. For example, the airline code for American Airlines is 001, and the airline code for United Airlines is 016. Eventually, three-letter IATA codes will replace the two-letter carrier codes presently used. For example, the three-letter code FIN will replace the two-letter carrier code AY, now used for Finnair.

The following are examples of carrier and airline codes for major international carriers.

| | | | |
|---|---|---|---|
| AA | AAL | 001 | American Airlines |
| AF | AFR | 057 | Air France |
| AY | FIN | 105 | Finnair |
| AZ | AZA | 055 | Alitalia |
| BA | BAW | 125 | British Airways |
| CO | COA | 005 | Continental Airlines |
| DL | DAL | 006 | Delta Air Lines |
| IB | IBE | 075 | Iberia |
| JL | JAL | 131 | Japan Airlines |
| KL | KLM | 074 | KLM Royal Dutch Airlines |
| LH | DLH | 220 | Lufthansa German Airlines |
| OS | AUA | 257 | Austrian Airlines |
| SK | SAS | 117 | Scandinavian (SAS) |
| SU | AFL | 555 | Aeroflot |
| UA | UAL | 016 | United Airlines |
| US | USA | 037 | U.S. Airways |

**Encoding an Airline**

The entry code W/-AL is used to encode an airline, as follows:

W/-AL<Carrier>

**Example**
W/-ALAER LINGUS

This example would be used to determine the carrier code for Aer Lingus.

**Decoding an Airline**

The entry code W/* is used to decode an airline code, as follows:

W/*<Carrier code>

**Example**
W/*AS

This example would be used to determine the name of the airline that has the carrier code AS.

4

## Equipment Codes

Each type of passenger aircraft is indicated by a three-letter equipment code. For example, 747 is the equipment code for Boeing 747, and D10 is the code for McDonnell Douglas DC-10. Some passenger aircraft, such as the 727, DC-10, or L-1011, have more than one model. For example, three basic models of the 727 are used for passenger transportation, including the 727, 727-100, and 727-200. Equipment codes are used in flight availability displays to indicate the type of aircraft used on each flight. The following are examples of various equipment codes:

| | |
|---|---|
| A3B | Airbus Industrie A-300B |
| DC9 | McDonnell-Douglas DC-9 |
| D10 | McDonnell-Douglas DC-10 |
| D9S | McDonnell-Douglas DC-9 Super Jet |
| L10 | McDonnell-Douglas MD-80 |
| 310 | Airbus Industrie A-310 |
| 320 | Airbus Industrie A-320 |
| 733 | Boeing 737-300 |
| 737 | Boeing 737 |
| 73S | Boeing 737-200 |
| 747 | Boeing 747 |
| 757 | Boeing 757 |

The equipment code 73S represents a special configuration of the 737 aircraft. The S indicates that the airplanes have been configured for additional passenger seating. These specially configured aircraft are commonly referred to as "stretch jets." Similarly, the code 73M indicate a "multiple" configuration, designed to transport cargo as well as passengers.

## Encoding Aircraft Equipment

The entry code W/EQ- is used to encode aircraft equipment, as follows:

W/EQ-<Equipment>

### Example
W/EQ-FOKKER F27

This example would be used to determine the equipment code for the Fokker F27 aircraft.

## Decoding Aircraft Equipment

The entry code W/EQ* is used to decode an equipment code, as follows:

W/EQ*<Equipment code>

### Example
W/EQ*M80

This example would be used to determine the aircraft equipment for the code M80.

# Review

1. Assume your ID code is 15432. Write the entry to sign on in work area A.

2. What entry is used to sign out from all work areas?

3. Write the entry to determine the airline code for Alitalia.

4. What entry would be used to decode the airline code CX?

5. Write the entry to decode the city code KHI.

6. Write the entry to display the city code for Seoul.

7. What entry will display the airport code for Gatwick?

8. Write the entry to display the equipment code for Fokker aircraft.

9. What entry would be used to decode the equipment code M80?

10. Write the entry to encode the airline Lufthansa.

# Flight Availability

## Objectives

*After completing this unit, you should be able to do the following:*

1. Sign in and sign out.
2. Display flight availability for a specified departure date and time.
3. Determine the origin and destination airports, departure time, arrival time, aircraft, meal service, flight number, and number of stopping points.
4. Display return, additional, and original availability.
5. Display connecting flights.
6. Change the date or time of an existing availability display.
7. Display availability by arrival time, class of service, or carrier.
8. Obtain a direct-access availability display from a carrier's reservation system.

The term **itinerary** refers to all the origin, destination, and intermediate points in a trip. Each portion of the itinerary is referred to as a **segment**. As an example, consider the following trip:

1. LAX - BOS
2. BOS - LAX

This example includes two flight segments. The first segment in the itinerary is called the originating or outbound segment, and the first point is called the originating point. In this example, Los Angeles (LAX) is the originating point, and Boston (BOS) is the turn-around point or destination. The flight that returns from the destination to the originating point is called the return flight. If a trip involves a connection, a separate segment is included in the itinerary for each connecting flight. For example, assume a passenger will travel from London to San Francisco, connecting in Chicago. After attending a meeting in San Francisco, he will be return on a nonstop flight to London. This passenger's itinerary will consist of the following air segments:

1. SFO - CHI
2. CHI - LON
3. LON - SFO

In this example, the passenger will depart from San Francisco (SFO), disembark in Chicago (CHI), and then board another flight to London (LON). The Chicago-London portion of the trip is a separate segment.

A point in a connection where a change of aircraft occurs is called a connecting point. Any point that is not a connecting point in an air itinerary is called a stopover point. In this example, Chicago is a connecting point, and London is a stopover point. The first city or airport in a flight segment is the departure or origin point, and the second city or airport is the arrival or destination point. Together, the departure point and arrival point form a "city pair."

A city pair availability display is a current list of regularly scheduled flights that operate between two specified points. To obtain an availability display, the agent must input the date of travel and the origin and destination points.

**Date Format**

Because flight schedules change frequently, it is important to specify the departure date when requesting availability. Dates are entered as codes, with the day entered as one or two digits and the month as a three-letter abbreviation. For example, 17 July is entered as 17JUL, and 3 December may be entered as either 3DEC or 03DEC.

**Displaying Availability**

The entry code for flight availability is the digit 1. This entry has the following format:

1<Date><City Pair><Departure Time>

**Example:**
110SEPCHIBOS10A

If a city is served by multiple airports, inputting the city code will display flights for all airports in the metropolitan area, whereas the airport code will display only flights for that airport. The time may be input in 12-hour format using A for "A.M." and P for "P.M.", or in 24-hour format.

*Response:*

```
10SEP  FRI    ORD/CDT      BOS/EDT‡1
1AA 1724 F7 Y7 B7 H7 Q7 ORDBOS 6  950A  111P S80 L 0 DCA /E
         G7 V7 K7 I7 O7 W7 M7 Z7
2AA 1198 F7 Y7 B7 H7 Q7 ORDBOS 6 1015A  141P S80 L 0 DCA /E
         G7 V7 K7 I7 O7 W7 M7 Z7
3UA  514 F9 A6 Y9 B9 M9 ORDBOS 7 1144P  253P 72S L 0 DCA /E
         H9 Q9 V9 W9 S9 T9 K9 L9 G9
4UA  518 F9 A9 Y9 B9 M9 ORDBOS 5 1245P  512P 757 S 0 DCA /E
         H9 Q9 V9 W9 S9 T9 K9 L9 G9
5UA  510 F5 A2 Y9 B9 M9 ORDBOS 8  144P  600P 733 L 0 X6 DCA /E
         H9 Q9 V9 W9 S9 T9 K9 L9 G9
6AA  528 F2 Y7 B7 H7 Q7 ORDBOS 8  140P  602P 100 L 0 DCA /E
         G7 V7 K7 I7 O7 W7 M7
  |    |              |        |    |    |   | | | |
  1    2              3        4    5    6   7 8 9 10
```

| 1 Carrier | 6 Arrival time |
|---|---|
| 2 Flight number | 7 Equipment code |
| 3 Seat quota | 8 Meal service |
| 4 Departure/arrival points | 9 Stops |
| 5 Departure time | 10 Direct Connect indicator |

The first line of the display indicates the departure date, day of the week, board point, off point, and time difference. In the example above, the U.S. time zone is displayed for each point. The lines below the header are flight listings. Each flight listing is numbered on the left. Up to six flights may be displayed in each availability screen.

The first column gives the two-letter carrier code for each flight. The flight number is given to the right of the carrier code. To the right of the flight number are several columns consisting of a letter and a number. These columns indicate the number of seats that can be sold in each class of service. The letter indicates the class, and the number indicates the number of seats. This information is called the **seat quota**. The first 5 classes are shown after the flight number, and additional classes are displayed on a separate line below.

The classes offered on each flight vary, depending on the carrier, type of aircraft, route, and other factors. The maximum number that will be displayed for each class depends on the carrier's agreement with SABRE. More seats may actually be available than the maximum number displayed.

To the right of the seat quota are the origin point and destination point. Note that the applicable airport code is shown for each point. The digit after the destination point indicates the **on-time performance**. The digit 6 indicates that the flight departs and arrives on time from 60 to 70 percent of the time. The on-time indicator is displayed only in North American displays. Note in this display that the flight times are in the 12-hour format. The time format may be set or changed by the agency. The 24-hour format is commonly used in Europe, Asia, and Africa, whereas the 12-hour format is the most often used in North America.

The scheduled arrival time is shown to the right of the departure time. In this example, the times are in 12-hour format.

The equipment code for each flight is shown to the right of the arrival time. Meal service The meal service code for each flight is shown to the right of the equipment code:

B   Full breakfast          D   Dinner
V   Continental breakfast   S   Snack
L   Lunch

If no meal code is displayed, meal service is not provided on the flight.

The number on the right of the meal service code indicates the number of intermediate stops. Any exceptions to the frequency of operation are indicated to the right of the stops. The frequency of operation refers to the days of the week on which a flight operates. The frequency exception indicates any days on which the flight does not operate. Days of the week are indicated by the following digits:

1       Monday          2   Tuesday
3       Wednesday       4   Thursday
5       Friday          6   Saturday
7       Sunday

For example, X6 indicates that a flight does not operate on Saturday.

The code DCA indicates a Direct Connect Availability carrier. The availability information is obtained directly from the carrier's system. If seats are booked, the reservation is made simultaneously on the carrier's system, as well.

The link status may be one of the following:

DCA    Direct Connect Availability
DC     Direct Connect Sell
AB     Answer Back
AT     Answer Back/Total Access
TA     Total Access

If seats are booked with a Direct Connect airline, the reservation is made simultaneously on the carrier's system. When a reservation is booked with an Answer Back participant, the segment is transmitted by Sabre to the carrier, which then confirms the booking. Seats can be booked directly on the system of a Total Access airline by means of a special entry format, which you will learn later.

**Connecting Flight Segments**

Assume an agent has obtained the following display:

```
19SEP   SUN   MEM/CDT       LAS/PDT-2
1NW      979 F9 Y9 B9 M9 MEMLAS 4   820P   951P 320 0 DCA
             H9 Q9 V0 K0
2NW      777 F5 Y9 B0 M0 MEMLAS 9   840A   105P 757 SL 1 DCA
             H0 Q0 V0 K0
3DL     2015 F7 A7 Y7 B7 MEMDFW 3   115P   240P 72S S/S/ 0 DCA
             M7 H7 Q7 K7 L0
4DL      845 F7 A7 Y7 B7     LAS 7  330P   413P 757 S 0 DCA
             M7 H7 Q7 K7 L0
5CO/NW  6085 A9 D9 F9 Y9 MEMIAH     155P   331P D9S 0 DCA
             H9 K9 B9 V9 Q5 T5
6CO        5 A9 D9 F4 Y9     LAS N  515P   615P 72S D/D/D/S 0 DCA
             H9 K9 B5 V0 Q0 T0
```

The flights in lines 3 and 4 are connecting flights. DL 2015 departs from MEM to DFW, where passengers must transfer to DL 845, which continues to LAS. The origin point of the continuing flight is omitted, indicating that is the same as the destination point of the previous segment. Note the flight in line 5 has two carrier codes, indicating a code-sharing or joint venture flight.

**Return Availability**

After flight availability has been obtained, the following format may be used to display flights for the return trip:

1R<Return Date><Departure Time>

**Example**
1R23SEP2P

This example will display return flights on 23 September, departing at about 2P. If the date is omitted, the display will default to the same date as the original availability entry.

**Additional Availability**

In many cases, more flights exist than can be displayed on one screen. To display additional flights, the following entry may be input:

     1*

**Changing the Time**

After city pair availability has been requested, availability may be displayed for an alternate departure time, by means of the following format:

1*<Alternate Time>

**Example:**
1*2P

The system responds by displaying availability for flights departing as close as possible to the specified time.

**Changing the Date**

After city pair availability has been requested, an alternate date can be specified as follows:

1<Alternate Date>

**Example:**
121MAY

Sabre responds by displaying availability on the specified date, using the same city pair requested in the most recent availability entry.

  To move the date forward one day, the following entry may be used:

     1‡1

To display availability for the same city pair three days earlier, the following entry may be used:

     1-3

When the date is moved forward or back, an alternate departure time may also be specified, as follows:

     1-7*10A

The example above will move the date back seven days and display flights departing around 10A.

## Changing the Departure or Arrival Point

The entry code 1*D may be used to change only the departure point of an existing availability display, as follows:

1*DMIA

This example above will change the departure point to Miami. The arrival point will remain the same as in the existing availability display. The entry code 1*A may be used to change only the arrival point, as follows:

1*AICT

The example above will change the arrival point to Wichita.

## Original Availability

To redisplay the original availability display, the following entry may be used:

1*OA

When this entry is input, the system redisplays the availability display that was obtained before any follow-up entries were input.

## Specifying a Connecting Point

A connecting point can be specified as follows:

12OCTLAXPAR09AORD

The connecting point is input at the end of the availability entry. The example above will display connections on 20 October from LAX to PAR, departing around 0900 and connecting at ORD. A minimum connecting time may also be specified, as follows:

12OCTLAXPAR0900ORD120

The example above specifies a minimum connecting time of 120 minutes.

A normal availability display can also be modified to show only flights via a specified connecting point. For example, assume the following availability entry has been input:

124APRDFWHNL10A

The example above will display all flights departing on 24 April from Dallas to Honolulu departing around 10A. The following entry will change the display to show only connections via San Francisco:

1SFO

After connecting flights have been requested, the following entry will change the display to the original format:

> 1*ORIG

Note that this entry can only be made after connections have been requested.

**Specifying an Arrival Time**

The arrival time may be specified as follows:

> 122OCTATLSTL/2P

Note that a slash (/) is typed before the desired arrival time. The arrival time can also be specified in a return availability entry, as follows:

> 1R27OCT/4P

The example above requests return availability on 27 October, arriving around 4P.

**Specifying a Class of Service**

A class of service may be specified as follows:

> 112DECSTLPAR-B

Note that a dash (-) is typed before the class of service. This entry will display availability only in B class.

An existing display can be modified to show a specific class as follows:

> 1-Q

This example will display only availability in Q class.

**Specifying a Carrier**

A carrier may be specified as follows:

> 118SEPSFOHNL0900‡UA

Note that a cross (‡) is typed before the carrier code. This entry will display only United flights.

Both the carrier and class may be specified as follows:

> 118SEPSFOHNL9A‡UA-C

## Nonstop/Direct Flights

The option /D may be included in an availability entry to show only direct flights, as follows:

118SEPSEAHNL0900/D

A direct flight is any flight that does not have a change of flight number at an intermediate connecting point.

## Last Seat Availability

The Total Access function may be used to obtain data directly from the reservation system of a Total Access or Answer Back/Total Access airline. The Total Access display will show the actual number of seats in each class. This type of display is referred to as last seat availability.

The following format is used to change an existing availability display to a Total Access display:

1 ¤<Carrier>

## Example
1 ¤SA

The example above will change the display to a Total Access display based on information obtained from the South African reservation system. Sabre responds as follows:

```
SA RESPONSE
 7SA 202 F0 J7 C7 Z0 Y7 M7 B7 K7 H7 JFKJNB 1120A  755A‡1 744 0
         S7 Q7 T7 V7 L7
 8SA7017 F4 J4 C4 Y4 K4              JFKMIA  920A 1223P   767 0
 9SA 204 F2 J7 C7 Z0 Y7 M7 B7 K7 H7    JNB  500P  340P‡1 744 1
         S7 Q7 T7 V7 L7
10SA7310 F4 Y4 K4                   JFKMIA 1216P  312P    AB6 0
11SA 204 F2 J7 C7 Z0 Y7 M7 B7 K7 H7    JNB  500P  340P‡1 744 1
         S7 Q7 T7 V7 L7
12SA7314 F4 Y4 K4                   EWRMIA 1253P  350P    757 0
13SA 204 F2 J7 C7 Z0 Y7 M7 B7          JNB  500P  340P‡1 744 1
_MD TO SEE MORE
```

A Total Access display remains in the agent's work area for approximately two minutes. After that, the display is replaced by a normal availability display.

The line numbers in a total access availability display always start with line 7 and may reach as high as 16, whereas the lines in a normal Sabre display are always numbered from 1 to 6.

A Total Access availability display may also be obtained as follows:

112JULNYCJNB10A¤SA

In this entry, ¤ is typed before the carrier code to link with the airline's system.

## Specific Flight Availability

Availability may also be checked on a specific flight, if the carrier and flight number are known. The following format is used for this purpose:

1<Carrier><Flight><Class><Date><City pair>

### Example
1UA440Y10MAYLGAMIA

The example above requests availability on UA 440 in Y class, departing 10MAY from LGA to MIA. Only airport codes may be used in this entry. If the requested class is sold out, an availability display will be shown, so that an alternate class or flight may be selected. The response may be one of the following:

| | |
|---|---|
| AS | Flight is available to sell. |
| CR | Flight is closed/seats may be requested. |
| CN | Flight does not operate. |
| CL | Flight is closed/seats may be waitlisted. |
| CC | Flight is closed/waitlist is closed. |
| NO AVAIL | Availability is not maintained for the requested carrier. |

# Review

Write the correct entry for each of the following:

1. Display availability from Cleveland (CLE) to Raleigh-Durham (RDU), departing at 1 PM on 19 March.

2. Display additional availability.

3. Change the departure time to 3 PM.

4. Change the departure date to 16 July.

5. Display return availability on 29 June, departing at 11 AM.

6. Display only direct flights on 24 May from Minneapolis (MSP) to Amsterdam (AMS) departing at about 2 PM.

7. Display availability only in C class on 30 April from Sydney (SYD) to Los Angeles (LAX).

8. Link with the SA reservation system to display availability from Miami (MIA) to Cape Town (CPT) departing on 12 February.

9. Display return availability at 6 PM on 27 February.

10. Display connections on 18 May from Atlanta (ATL) to Seattle (SEA) departing at 8 AM and connecting in Denver (DEN).

11. Display availability in Y class on AA 331 departing on 18 October from DFW to LAX.

# Selling Air Segments

## Objectives

*After completing this unit, you should be able to do the following:*

1. Sell air segments from a flight availability display.
2. Interpret an air segment.
3. Identify the status/action code for a confirmed segment.
4. Sell a connection from a flight availability display.
5. Waitlist a seat request.
6. Sell or waitlist seats directly by flight number.
7. Book an open segment.
8. Input a passive air segment booked directly with the airline.
9. Input a surface (ARNK) segment.

Citizens of the ancient Roman Empire could purchase a first-class or second-class ticket to travel by chariot over the Appian Way. The ticket was accompanied by a document called an *itinerarium*, listing all the places where the passenger was entitled to travel. The term **itinerary** is still used today to identify the origin, destination, and all the stopping points on a traveler's journey. Each portion of the itinerary is referred to as a segment.

Booking an airline reservation is referred to as selling an air segment. If the requested seats are not available, the reservations may be placed on a waitlist. If other passengers who hold confirmed seats later cancel their reservations, the waitlisted seats may be confirmed. The entry code 0 is used to sell an air segment.

## Selling From Availability

When an availability display has been obtained, seats may be sold on a selected flight by means of the following entry:

0<Seats><Class><Line>

**Example:**
01Y1

The digit 0 is followed by the number of seats, the class of service, and the line number for the desired flight. The number of seats may not exceed the number shown in the display for the requested class of service. In general, a maximum of 7 or 9 seats may be sold on a flight if the Direct Connect status is DCA (unless the actual number shown is less than the desired number of seats). On some carriers, a maximum of 4 seats may be sold, and, if fewer than 4 seats are available, 0 is displayed.

If the agent attempts to sell more than the maximum number displayed, the seats will be requested from the airline. If the desired flight and class are sold out, a request for seats may be placed on the carrier's waitlist for that flight.

The class code must be one of the valid classes of service in the availability display--for example, F (first class), C (business class), Y (coach), B (discount coach), etc. If the number of seats requested exceeds the maximum number displayed, the booking will not be confirmed immediately, and the seats will be requested from the carrier.

Example

Assume a client wants to travel on 10 September from Chicago to Boston. The agent first displays availability as follows:

    110SEPCHIBOS

Sabre responds as follows:

```
10SEP  WED   CHI/CST   BOS/EST‡1
1AA 152 F7 Y7 M7 W7 H7 B7 Q7    ORDBOS 8   700A 1050A D10 S 0 DCA /E
2DL 296 F7 Y7 H7 B7 M7 Q7 L7    ORDBOS 8   815A 1113A 72S B 0 DCA
3AA 580 F7 Y7 M7 W7 H7 B7 Q7    ORDBOS 7  1003A  101P D10 S 0 DCA /E
4UA 166 F9 Y9 B9 M9 H9 Q9 V9    ORDBOS 9  1235P  508P 73S L 1 DCA /E
5AA1724 F7 Y7 M7 W7 H7 B7 Q7    ORDBOS 9  1250P  411P 767 L 0 DCA /E
6UA 100 F9 Y9 B9 M9 H9 Q9 V9    ORDBOS 7   200P  513P D10 S 0 DCA /E
```

Assume the client prefers the American Airlines flight departing at 1250P. The agent books the air segment as follows:

    01Y5

This entry will book 1 seat in Y class on the flight in line 5 of the availability display.

Each flight in the itinerary is listed on a separate line and is referred to as an air segment. Besides air segments, the itinerary may also include auxiliary segments, such as car rental or hotel reservations.

Each air segment consists of the following items:

```
1 AA1724Y 10SEP 1 ORDBOS SS2 1250P   411P /DCAA /E
|   |         |   |    |    ||   |      |     |
A   B         C   D    E    FG   H      I     J
```

| | | | |
|---|---|---|---|
| A | Segment number | F | Segment status |
| B | Carrier, flight, and class | G | Number of seats |
| C | Departure date | H | Departure time |
| D | Day of week | I | Arrival time |
| E | Departure/arrival points | J | Direct Connect indicator |

If the segment was booked with a Direct Connect (or Direct Connect Availability) participant, the code /DC is displayed, followed by the carrier code, when the itinerary is redisplayed. If the segment is eligible for electronic ticketing, the code /E is displayed on the right.

## Selling Connections

The following entry is used to sell connecting flight segments in the same class:

    01Y4*

The example above will sell one seat in Y class on all legs of a connection beginning in line 2.

*Response:*

```
 1 DL2015Y 12MAR 2 MEMDFW SS1   225P   240P
 2 DL 845Y 12MAR 2 DFWLAX SS1   330P   413P
```

To book connecting flights in different classes of service, the agent inputs the class and line number of each leg, as follows:

    01C4Y5

This entry would be used to book the flight in line 4 in C class and the flight in line 5 in Y class.

## Displaying the Itinerary

When air segments are booked, the following entry may be used to display the complete itinerary:

    *I

The asterisk key (*) is referred to as the Display key. When the itinerary is displayed, the segments are listed in the order in which they were booked, as follows:

```
 1 UA 962Y 12AUG 1 SFOLHR SS1   110P   610A T /DCUA /E
 2 UA 981Y 19AUG 1 LHRLAX SS1  1000A   832A /DCUA /E
 3 UA 394Y 24AUG 6 LAXSFO SS1  1005A  1100A /DCUA /E
```

In this example, the flight in line 1 arrives on Tuesday, as indicated by the day of the week code displayed after the arrival time.

## Selling by Carrier and Flight Number

Seats can be sold on a specified flight without an availability display, if the carrier, flight number, and departure date are known.

The entry code NN is used in direct-sell entries, as follows:

0<Carrier><Flight><Class><Date><Origin><Destination>NN<Seats>

**Example**

0DL650Y27AUGATLORDNN2

The applicable airport code must be used for a multi-airport city. The action code NN (need/need) is input before the number of seats. If the class or flight is sold out, Sabre will present an availability display for the same city pair, so that an alternative class or flight may be selected. Sabre responds as follows:

```
0DL650Y27AUGATLORDNN2    950A 1250P 3 S SEG 1 SS Y
```

The flight times, day of the week, meal code, segment number, status, and class are displayed in the response. Note the segment status is SS (sold/sold), indicating that the booking will be confirmed by the carrier. If the number of seats exceeds the carrier's seat quota, the segment status will remain NN until the seats are confirmed by the airline.

# Waitlisted Segments

Each carrier maintains a waiting list, or waitlist, for flights that are sold out. Passengers who want seats on the flight are placed on the list, in case other passengers who hold confirmed reservations happen to cancel their reservations.

The secondary code LL is used to place waitlist seats, as follows:

02Y4LL

The example above will waitlist two seats in Y class on the flight in line 4 of the availability display. Sabre responds as follows:

```
1 AS 157Y 18NOV 1 ANCSEA LL1   755A 1145A /E
```

Note that the segment status is LL, indicating that the seats will be waitlisted. When the transaction is ended, the segment status will be changed to HL, signifying that the space has been waitlisted. In case the waitlisted segment is not confirmed later, a confirmed reservation should also be booked for the same routing.

**Waitlisting Seats on a Specified Flight**

To waitlist with a direct-sell entry, the agent types the waitlist action code LL instead of NN, as follows:

0AA242Y16APRDFWLAXLL2

Sabre responds as follows:

```
1040A 1225A 5 S SEG 1 LL Y /E
```

Note the segment status is LL, indicating that the seats will be placed on the carrier's waitlist.


## Open Segments

An open segment is an unspecified flight on a specified carrier. To book an open segment, use the direct-sell format to input the data, but type the word OPEN in place of the flight number, and use the action code DS (Desire Seats) before the number of seats. An open segment does not necessarily require a travel date. However, to price the ticket, an estimated date should be included.

As an example, assume that a client has booked one seat in Y class from FRA to JFK. He would like to return on LH on 12 March, but does not yet know the exact departure time. The following entry may be used to book the open segment in C class:

0LHOPENC12MARJFKFRADS1

Sabre responds with the following information:

```
SEG 2 OPEN C 12MAR JFKFRA DS1
```

Note that, in this example, an outbound segment was booked previously, and, thus, the open segment is segment 2.


## Passive Segments

Occasionally, an air segment must be booked directly with a carrier by telephone, rather than through Sabre. The direct-sell format can be used to record the segment in the itinerary for the passenger's information. This type of reservation is called a passive segment.

The action code GK or BK may be used to input a passive segment, as in the following example:

0SQ865Y22SEPHKGSINGK2

A passive segment is for information only and is input only if the reservation was booked by a means other than through Sabre. To indicate a passive waitlisted segment, the action code BL or GL may be used.

## Surface Segments

A surface segment is any segment in which the passenger will travel by a means other than air transportation. Examples of surface segments include travel by car, ship, or rail. Surface segments are not booked in an air itinerary. However, an ARNK segment is input to indicate surface travel when an air itinerary is interrupted.

ARNK is an abbreviation for "arrival unknown." Whenever the departure point of an air segment is different from the arrival point of the previous segment, an ARNK segment must be placed in the itinerary to maintain continuity.

For example, assume a client will travel from BOS to MIA by air. The passenger will travel by surface from MIA to FLL, before boarding a return flight to BOS. This itinerary includes the following segments:

1. BOS - MIA
2. ARNK
3. FLL - BOS

The arrival point of segment 1 is MIA, but the departure point of segment 2 is FLL. To maintain continuity in the itinerary, an ARNK segment is placed between the two air segments. The ARNK segment signifies that the trip is interrupted by another form of transportation.

# Review

1. Select by letter the correct entry to sell 3 first class seats on a flight in line 2.

     (a) 0F32
     (b) 03F2
     (c) 02F2
     (d) 02F3

2. Study the following entry, then answer the questions below.

     03Y2

(a) In what class is the segment being booked?

(b) How many seats will be sold?

(c) What is the applicable line number in the availability display?

3. Refer to the following availability display to answer questions (a) through (c):

```
12OCT   TUE    STL/CDT      LAX/PDT-2
1AA 2037 F7 Y7 B7 Q7 K7 STLLAX 7 1155A  200P   757 L/S 0 DCA
         V7 T7 H7 S7
2AA 2039 F7 Y7 B7 Q7 K7 STLLAX 5  215P  417P   M80 L/S 0 DCA
         V7 T7 H0 S0
3AA 2043 F7 Y7 B7 Q7 K7 STLLAX 6  843A 1040A   757 B/S 0 DCA
         V7 T7 H7 S7
4AA 2043 F7 Y7 B7 Q7 K7 STLLAX 4  540P  744P   757 D/S 0 DCA
         V7 T7 H7 S0
5AA 2161 F7 Y7 B7 Q7 K7 STLLAX 5  825P 1029P   757 S/  0 DCA
         V7 T7 H7 S7
```

(a) Write the entry to sell 4 seats in Y class on the flight that arrives at 10:40 AM.

(b) Write the entry to sell 2 seats in K class on the flight that departs at 5:40 PM.

(c) Write the entry to sell one seat in H class on the flight that departs at 8:35 PM.

4. Study the following itinerary segment to answer the questions below.

```
1 QF   1 Y 13JUL 3 MELLHR SS3  130P  655A Q /DCQF
```

(a) In what class of service are the seats booked?

(b) How many seats are booked?

(c) On what day of the week will the passengers depart?

(d) What is the departure point?

(e) What time is the flight scheduled to arrive at the arrival point?

5. Write the correct entry to sell one seat in C class on a connection starting in line 3.

6. Write the correct entry to sell 3 seats in C class on the first leg and in Y class on the second leg of a connection starting in line 5.

7. Write the entry to sell one seat in C class on BA 510 on 13 December from Los Angeles (LAX) to London Heathrow (LHR).

8. Write the correct entry to waitlist one passenger in Y class on UA 189 on 22 May from Chicago O'Hare (ORD) to San Francisco (SFO).

9. What term is used to describe a segment inserted in an itinerary to maintain continuity when the destination of one air segment is different from the origin of the next air segment?

10. What entry will enter the type of segment described in question 6 above in the itinerary?

11. Assume you booked a flight directly by phone with Sunflower Air (PI) and reserved 2 seats in S class on flight 14 from Nadi (NAN) to Savusavu (SVU) on 20 July. Write the entry input the passive segment.

12. Write the entry to book an open segment for one passenger in C class on United from Frankfurt (FRA) to Washington Dulles (IAD).

# Passenger Name Records

**Objectives**

*After completing this unit, you should be able to do the following:*

1. Identify the five mandatory parts of a passenger name record (PNR).
2. Input passenger names.
3. Input contact telephone numbers.
4. Input the ticketing arrangement.
5. Enter received-from information.
6. Redisplay the record.
7. End the transaction.

A passenger name record, or PNR, is a computer record of each reservation. The PNR has five mandatory parts, as follows:

1. Number of passengers and their names
2. Contact telephone numbers
3. Ticketing information
4. Received-from information
5. Itinerary

Each part that contains data about the passenger is referred to as a field. Each field has a label identifying the information stored in the field. The passenger data fields include the name, phone, ticketing, and received-from fields.

**Name Field**

The name field consists of one or more name items. Passenger names are grouped together by family name. All passengers who have the same family name are listed in each name item. A PNR may contain one or more name items--for example, parties with different family names.

**Phone Field**

The phone field contains contact telephone numbers for the reservation. The travel agency phone must be included in every PNR, but the record should also contain the client's business and/or home phone.

**Ticketing Field**

The ticketing field contains information or advice about passenger ticketing, such as the date on which tickets will be issued.

**Received-from Field**

The received-from field contains a record of the person who requested the reservation, such as the passenger or the passenger's secretary or spouse.

The passenger data may be entered in any order, but each entry must be made using the proper format. A PNR containing the mandatory parts, or data fields, is illustrated below.

```
    1.2HUNTER/RICHARD MR/LAUREN MRS
 1 UA  98Y 12OCT 2 SFOATL SS2  1050A  627P /DCUA /E
 2 UA 311Y 17OCT 7 ATLSFO SS2   335P  857P /DCUA /E
 TKT/TIME LIMIT -
   1.TAW11OCT/
 PHONES-
   1.SFO415-342-1661-A
   2.SFO415-451-7823-B
   3.SFO415-745-2003-H
 RECEIVED FROM - MR
```

**Creating a PNR**

To create a PNR, the travel consultant or ticketing agent inputs information into the data fields. The itinerary and the name, phone, ticketing, and received-from fields must be completed before the reservation can be stored. Each field has a code called an identifier, consisting of one or more letters, numbers, or symbols.

**Storing a PNR**

To store the PNR, the agent "ends" the transaction by typing "E" or "ET" and then presses the Enter key. When a transaction is ended, the PNR is transmitted to the CRS for storage and the agent's work area is erased. A transaction cannot be ended unless the PNR has an itinerary and data in the name, phone, ticketing, and received-from fields.

**Ignoring the Transaction**

To erase the work area without storing the current PNR, the agent can "ignore" the transaction by typing "I" and then pressing the Enter key. When a transaction is ignored, any data in the agent's work area is erased.

**Retrieving a PNR**

A PNR that has been previously ended may be retrieved from storage. When a record has been retrieved, it may be changed or updated before it is saved again. A PNR that is held in the work area must be ended or ignored before another record can be displayed. Any time a record is created or changed, an entry must be made to the received-from field, to indicate the person who requested the booking, service, or change.

# Name Field

The basic name entry consists of the passenger's family name (last name), given name or initial, and an identifying title. The field identifier that is used to input name entries is the dash key (–). Name entries have the following format:

–<Family name>/<Given Name or Initial> <Title>

## Example:
–LINDBERGH/CHARLES MR

This example will input the name for Mr. Charles Lindbergh. The title serves to identify the sex and marital status of the passenger, as well as any special occupation, as in the case of a military or religious title. In this case, the title MR identifies the passenger as a male over 12 years of age.

## Examples of Titles Used in Name Entries

| | |
|---|---|
| MR | Mr. (Male, 13 years or older) |
| MRS | Mrs. (Female spouse) |
| MS | Ms. (Female, 13 years or older, marital status unknown) |
| MSTR | Master (Male, 12 years or younger) |
| MISS | Miss (Female, 12 years or younger) |
| DR | Doctor |

## Multiple Passengers with the Same Family name

Multiple passengers with the same family name are input as follows:

–2SHELLEY/RAYMOND MR/MARY MRS

The number of passengers with the same family name is typed after the family name. Note that a slash (/) is typed before each initial.

## Examples of Name Entries

Assume a passenger, Mr. George Byron, will travel unaccompanied. The passenger name is input as follows:

–BYRON/GEORGE MR

Now suppose the reservation is for Mr. George Byron and Mrs. Charlotte Byron. In this case, the name item would be input as follows:

–2BRYON/GEORGE MR/CHARLOTTE MRS

Now assume Mr. and Mrs. Byron will travel with their son, D. Byron. The title MSTR identifies a male child under the age of 12, as in the following entry:

–3BYRON/GEORGE MR/CHARLOTTE MRS/D MSTR

The initial, rather than the full given name, is normally input for children of age 15 or under.

### Guidelines for Name Entries

1. Verify the spelling of each family name.
2. Separate the first initial from the family name with a slash (/).
3. Identify each passenger with a title. Type a period between the initial and title.
4. Separate each initial and title from the others with a slash (/).

### Multiple Name Entries

The end-item character (Σ) may be used to input multiple entries simultaneously.

As an example, assume you wish to input the name entry for Mr. Charles Black along with that for Mr. Arnold White. The name entries may be combined as follows:

–BLACK/CHARLES MRΣ–WHITE/ARNOLD MR

Observe that this entry is actually two separate name entries connected by an End-Item.

### Examples of Name Entries

–CARSON/LAWRENCE MR
–2BLOOMFIELD/MICHAEL MR/ANNE MRS
–4BEAMAN/RONALD MR/JOAN MRS/A MSTR/T MISS
–JUDSON/CHRIS MRΣ–MASTERS/WILLIAM MR

## Phone Field

The field identifier 9 is used to input contact telephone numbers. The travel agency phone is entered before any other phones and must appear in every PNR. Contact phones are input as follows:

9<Area Code>–<Phone>–<Location>

**Example:**
9602-934-7728-B

In this example, the location indicator B signifies a business phone. The location indicator may be one of the following:

| | |
|---|---|
| A | Travel agency |
| B | Business |

H    Home or hotel

If the city code is different from the agency location, the city code may be typed before the area code. If the city code is omitted, Sabre inserts the agency's local city code automatically.

**Guidelines For Phone Entries**

1. Input the travel agency phone first.
2. Identify the location with the applicable locator indicator.
3. The travel agency name or the agent's given name or initials may be input with the agency phone for identification.

**Examples of Phone Entries**

9415-927-6872-A/JETSET TVL
9SNA909-265-1919-B
9315-823-1127-H

**Identifying the Passenger**

When a reservation is made for multiple travelers with different family names, each business phone and home phone should be identified by the name of the respective passenger. As an example, assume a PNR includes two passengers, Mr. L. Glenn and Mr. C. Stein. In the business phone entry for passenger Glenn, the family name should be included, as follows:

9902-551-1238-B/GLENN

**Multiple Phone Numbers**

Multiple phone items can be input simultaneously by means of an end-item, as follows:

9213-554-1798-BΣ9213-556-7293-H

Note that the phone field identifier 9 must be typed for each phone item. Remember that the agency phone should be input before any other phones.

# Ticketing Field

The ticketing field is used to indicate the ticketing arrangements requested by the passenger. For example, if tickets will be printed on a future date, the ticketing date is input in this field. The field identifier 7 is used to input information in the ticketing field, as follows:

7<Ticketing Advice Code>

**Example:**
7TAW18MAY/

The example above will cause the PNR to appear in a special electronic holding area, called the automatic ticketing queue, on 18 May. The code TAW is used to arrange automatic ticketing on a specified date. Note that a slash (/) is typed after the date.

The code T-A is used to indicate that the PNR is ticketed, as follows:

7T-A/24JUN

This example would be input to indicate that the PNR has been ticketed by the travel agency-for instance, if handwritten tickets have been issued. Other advice codes include TAX (teleticketing request) and PTA (prepaid ticket advice).

**Examples of Ticketing Arrangements**

| | |
|---|---|
| 7TAW12JUN/ | Ticketing arrangement for 12 June |
| 7TAX8FEB/ | Teleticketing request for 8 February |
| 7TAVGO/TAW26MAR | Tour ticketing arrangement |

The entry code 8 is used to indicate a time limit, as follows:

830

This entry indicates that the ticket must be purchased at least 30 minutes prior to departure.


# Received-from Field

The received-from information is a mandatory item in every PNR. The field identifier 6 is used to input information in the received-from field, as follows:

6<Text>

**Example:**
6P

The received-from entry indicates the person who requested the service. In this example, the abbreviation P stands for "passenger," denoting that the passenger requested the reservation. If someone other than the passenger requested the service, the title and family name--or family name, initial, and title--should be input. The text portion of the entry is freeform, but consistency and clarity are important.

**Examples of Received-from Entries**

Assume that a reservation was requested by the passenger's assistant, Ms Bloomfield. The received-from information may be input as follows:

6MS BLOOMFIELD

There are no strict rules for received-from entries. Various agencies have different procedures for "receiving" the PNR. In general, the minimum acceptable input for the received-from field is "6P".

**Redisplaying the PNR**

As information is entered into the various fields, the data is held temporarily in the agent's work area. The data is rearranged automatically whenever the record is redisplayed, as follows:

    *A

**Ending the Transaction**

When information has been input in the mandatory fields, the agent may end the transaction to store the record. The following entry is input to end the transaction:

    E

This action is commonly referred to as "end transact." An end-item may be used to input a passenger data item and end the transaction with one entry. For example, the following format may be used to input the received-from item and end transact:

    6PΣE

When the transaction is ended, a six-character code, called a record locator, is displayed. This code can be used to retrieve the PNR. You will learn how to retrieve PNRs later. Before the transaction is ended, the PNR must have a name field, itinerary, phone field, ticketing arrangement, and received-from field. The entry "ER" may be used to end the transaction and redisplay the PNR.

**Building a PNR**

Assume a client wants to travel from Los Angeles to Denver on 12 May. The travel consultant displays availability as follows:

    A12MAYLAXDEN

Sabre responds as follows:

```
 12MAY TUE   LAX/PDT    DEN/CDT╿2
1CO   62 F9 Y9 B9 Q9 M9 LAXDEN 8 630A   932A 72S B 0 DCA /E
         K9 H9 V9
2CO   86 F9 Y9 B9 Q9 M9 LAXDEN 9 710A 1017A 72S B 0 DCA /E
         K9 H9 V9
3UA 320 F9 Y9 B9 Q9 M9 LAXDEN 9 715A 1010A 73S B 0 DCA /E
         H9 V9
4HP2492 F7 Y7 B7 Q7 M7 LAXDEN 8 715A 1020A 727 0 DC
         K7 H7 V7
```

Let's say the client prefers the United  flight departing at 715A. The agent books the flight as follows:

01Y3

The client would like to return on 17 May, departing at 2 PM. The agent displays return availability as follows:

1R17MAY2P

The agent books the return segment as follows:

01Y1

To review the flight segments, the agent inputs the entry to display the itinerary, as follows:

*I

Sabre displays the segments as follows:

```
1 UA 320Y 12MAY 2 LAXDEN SS1   715A 1010A /DCUA /E
2 UA 347Y 17MAY 7 DENLAX SS1   235P  430P /DCUA /E
```

The agent verifies the spelling of the passenger's name and inputs the name field as follows:

-WHITMAN/WALTER MR

Next, the agent inputs the agency phone as follows:

9213-551-7284-A/DIANNE

The agent now asks the client for his business contact phone and then inputs the phone, as follows:

9213 555-7271-B

The agent also asks for the client's home phone and inputs the information as follows:

9213 555-2492-H

When a ticketing date has been arranged, the agent inputs the ticketing item, as follows:

7TAW10MAY /

To complete the PNR, the agent enters the received-from item, as follows:

6P

The abbreviation P indicates that the reservation was received from the passenger. To review the PNR, the agent displays all the fields as follows:

*A

Sabre displays the entire record, as follows:

```
   1.1WHITMAN/WALTER MR
1 UA 320Y 12MAY 2 LAXDEN SS1   715A 1010A /DCUA /E
2 UA 347Y 17MAY 7 DENLAX SS1   235P  430P /DCUA /E
TKT/TIME LIMIT
   1.TAW10MAY/
PHONES
   1.LAX213-555-3093-A/DIANNE
   2.LAX213-555-7271-B
   3.LAX213-555-2492-H
RECEIVED-FROM - P
```

The agent explains the itinerary to the client, verifying the carrier, flight, date, and departure time, and then inputs the entry to end the transaction, as follows:

E

Sabre responds as follows:

OK 1013 9SG5RB

Inputting Multiple Items

The end-item can be used to input multiple data items in one entry. (On PC keyboards, the comma (,) is used to type an end-item, which is displayed on the screen as Σ).
As an example, the following entry may be used to input two name items:

-MCGRAW/MAXWELL MRΣ-HILL/LAWRENCE MR

The end-item may be used to input several items in different fields, as in the following example:

-STEINBECK/JOHN MRΣ9907-555-2099Σ6P

# Review

1. What entry code is used to input a passenger's name?

2. Write the name entry for Mr. Thomas Moore.

3. Mr. Alan Clemson and his wife, Jane, will travel together. What entry would be used to input the name item?

4. Mr. Warren Lionel and Mrs. Mary Lionel will travel their children, Mstr. J. Lionel and Miss E. Lionel. Write the correct name entry.

5. Mr. Franz Steglitz will travel with Mrs. Beatrice Steglitz, Mrs. G. Steglitz, and Miss H. Steglitz. Write the correct name entry for these passengers.

6. What entry code is used to input a contact phone?

7. Assume the travel agency phone is 415-753-4332. Write the correct phone entry.

8. Assume you are creating a PNR for a passenger whose home phone is 305-640-2872. Write the correct phone entry.

9. Assume a client's business phone is 404-664-0987. Write the entry to input the phone.

10. What code is used to input information to the ticketing field?

11. Write the entry to arrange ticketing for 19 July.

12. What entry code is used to enter information in the received-from field?

13. What entry is often used to indicate that the passenger requested his or her own flight reservations?

14. Assume you are creating a PNR for a client whose flight reservations were made by his assistant, Mr. Poundstone. Write the received-from entry.

# Supplementary Data

**Objectives**

*After completing this unit, you should be able to do the following:*

1. Enter information in the remarks field.
2. Enter the form of payment.
3. Enter an OSI message.
4. Enter a special service request.
5. Identify common SSR codes.

The term supplementary data or supplemental data refers to additional information which may be required to complete a PNR. The following fields are used for this purpose: remarks, general facts, and AA Facts.

The remarks field is used to record any general information about the PNR. The form of payment and client address may also be entered in this field. The general facts field is used to communicate a message or service request to airline personnel other than the host (American Airlines). The AA Facts field is used only to send a message or request to American Airlines.

## PNR Remarks

The remarks field may be used to store notes, such as a reminder about some aspect of the reservation, or a message to another agent in the office. Any free-form text may be input in this field, and abbreviations are frequently used. The field identifier 5 is used to input remarks, as follows:

5<Text>

**Example:**
5PSGR WILL PICK UP TKTS BEFORE 3P

To illustrate, assume you are creating a PNR for a client who will travel abroad. You have advised the passenger of documents required for international travel. The phrase "ADVISED DOCUMENTS" is often used for this purpose, as in the following entry:

5ADVISED DOCUMENTS

Some agents might abbreviate this message as follows:

5ADVD DOCS

Although abbreviations are often used, it is important that the text is clear and concise. Remember that other agents might need to review the PNR.

**Form of Payment**

When the ticket is printed, the form of payment must be indicated, so that the proper information can be printed in the "form of payment" box. One way of fulfilling this requirement is to store the form of payment in the remarks field, as follows:

　　　5–CK

This entry indicates that the ticket will be purchased by check. Note that a dash (-) is typed before the form of payment.

If a credit card is used to purchase the ticket, the credit card type, account number, and expiration date must be input, as follows:

　　　5–*BA53O41122998710O22‡1218

In this example, BA indicates a Visa card. Note that a slash is typed before the expiration date, which consists of the digits for the month and year. The asterisk before the credit card code requests automatic approval.

The following credit card codes are used in form of payment entries:

| | |
|---|---|
| VI, BA | Visa |
| IK, MC, CA | Mastercard |
| AX | American Express |
| CB | Carte Blanche |
| DC | Diner's Club |
| DS | Discover |
| TP | Air travel card |
| AA | American Airlines travel card |

Note that multiple codes exist for Visa and Mastercard. The exact code that the system will accept depends on the issuer and account number. For example, BA is used for Visa cards issued by the Bank of America, and VI is used for most other issuers.

**Examples of Form of Payment Entries**

| | |
|---|---|
| 5–CASH | Cash |
| 5–CK | Bank check |
| 5–*AX3OO2365418872‡1118 | Credit card with expiration date |

# Client Addresses

The client address may also be input in the remarks field to indicate a mailing address or delivery address.

The entry code 5/ is used to input the client mailing adress. Each line of the address must be input on a separate line of the remarks field. The end-item may be used to input an entire address with one entry, as follows:

> 5/DR H MORROWΣ5/752 OAK STREETΣ5/LOS ANGELES CA 90102

Note that the entry code 5/ is typed with each line of the address.

## Agency Address

The entry code W– is used to input a travel agency address, as follows:

> W–LAKESIDE TRAVEL‡752 LAKE ST‡CHICAGO IL 60612

Note that a cross (‡) is typed before each succeeding line of the address.

## Invoice/Itinerary Remarks

The remarks field may also be used to store text information to print on the printed invoice or itinerary when tickets are issued.

### *Invoice Remarks*

Text entered in a PNR to print on the printed invoice is called an invoice remark. The entry code 5. is used to input invoice remarks as follows:

> 5.PAYMENT DUE IN 5 DAYS

The text portion of the entry is free-form. To input an invoice remark to print on multiple lines, separate each line with an end-item as follows:

> 5.HAVE A GREAT VACATIONΣ5.THANK YOU FOR USING ABC TRAVEL

### *Itinerary Remarks*

The entry code 5‡ is used to input text information to appear on the passenger itinerary when tickets are issued with a printed itinerary. The following is an example:

> 5‡MEET LIMOUSINE BY BAGGAGE CLAIM

## Other Service Information

Other Service Information, or Optional Service Information, (OSI) passes along information of an advisory nature to airline personnel. For example, if the passenger is elderly or has a physical handicap, airline personnel should be advised by means of an OSI message. The entry does not normally require any specific action or reply on the part of the airline. OSI entries may be used for any of the following:

1. Inform an airline of infant travel
2. Advise the airlines about VIP travel
3. Indicate an elderly passenger
4. Indicate a first-time air passenger
5. Send general information of an advisory nature

### OSI Entries

The field identifier for service information is the numeral 3. The entry code 3OSI is used to input OSI entries to carriers other than American Airlines, as follows:

3OSI  <Carrier Code> <Message>

**Example:**
3OSI UA ELDERLY PSGR

The example above would be input to advise United of an elderly passenger. An OSI entry to carriers other than American Airlines is referred to as a GFAX (general facts) OSI.

To illustrate, assume a very important passenger, Mr. P. Warner, the Swiss consul, will travel on a NW flight. The following entry may be used to alert the airline:

3OSI NW VIP SWISS CONSUL

The text portion of the entry is free-form, and abbreviations are commonly used, as in the entry above. In this example, "VIP" indicates a "Very Important Passenger." There are no strict rules governing the use of abbreviations in OSI messages, but consistency and clarity are important.

To indicate "all carriers" in the itinerary, type YY instead of a carrier code, as in the following example:

3OSI YY ELDERLY PSGR

This OSI message will be sent to all carriers in the itinerary, notifying them that the party includes a ten-year-old child. Note that the passenger is referenced by the appropriate title and initial. If multiple passengers have the same initial and title, the applicable surname should be included.

An OSI entry to American Airlines is referred to as an AFAX (AA facts) OSI. The entry code 4 is used to input AFAX OSI entries, as follows:

4OSI ELDERLY PSGR

AFAX entries are sent to American Airlines automatically, so the carrier code AA is not required.

**Examples of OSI Entries**

3OSI YY VIP SPANISH AMBASSADOR
3OSI  DL TVL W/INF
4OSI VIP FRENCH CONSUL

## Contact Details

It is recommended to send the client's mobile phone and e-mail address to the airline in an OSI message in case of a flight disruption. The service code CTCM is used to communicate the client's mobile phone, as follows:

3OSI <Carrier> CTCM.<Mobile phone>

**Example:**
3OSI UA CTCM.4157950627

Note that a dot (.) is typed before the mobile phone number. A language restriction may be included as follows:

> 3OSI DL CTCM.0114467266/FR

In this example, /FR indicates that the passenger speaks only French.

The service code CTCE is used to input a passenger's contact e-mail address, as follows:

> 3OSI UA CTCE.ADMIN//MYCOMPANY.COM

Note that the @ component of the e-mail address is typed as //.

## Special Service Requests

A Special Service Request (SSR) is sent to an airline to request special action or service. For example, if a passenger requests a special meal or requires a wheelchair to board or disembark the aircraft, an SSR request must be sent to the applicable airlines. The following are examples of typical situations requiring an SSR entry:

- Special meal requests
- Wheelchair service, or other handicapped needs
- Bassinet
- Personal assistance (e.g., for elderly or handicapped)
- Approval of pet transportation

Whereas an OSI entry merely passes along information, an SSR request requires a specific response from the airline(s).

**SSR Entries**

The field identifier 3 is used to input GFAX SSR entries, as follows: :

3<Request Code><Segment>-<Name Reference>

**Example:**
3VGML1

This example will transmit a service request to the carrier in segment 1. Most service items that can be requested with an SSR entry are identified with a four-letter request code.  In the example above, the code VGML is input to request a vegetarian meal.

If the service request applies to all air segments in the itinerary, the segment number may be omitted, as follows:

3BLND

This example requests assistance for a visually challenged (blind) passenger, for all segments.

**Name Reference**

If the reservation is for more than one traveler, the name reference must be included in the SSR entry (unless the service item is to be provided to all passengers in the PNR). Name reference is input as follows:

3VGML1-1.2

This example requests a vegetarian meal for the second passenger in the first name field. The service request will be transmitted to the carrier in segment 1.

To illustrate, assume a PNR has the following name items:

```
1.1JAMES/JOHN MR   2.1KIDD/WALTER MR   3.1CARSON/KEITH MR
```

Mr. Carson is visually challenged. When a reservation is booked for a passenger who is blind or deaf, an SSR entry should be input so that the airline can provide the proper level of service. The following entry will notify the carriers in all segments about Mr. Carson's disability:

3BLND-3.1

The entry code 4 is used to input a special service request for an American Airlines flight, as follows:

4VGML1-1.2

40

## Special Meal Requests

Only official meal codes may be used to request meals for passengers with special dietary restrictions or personal or religious preferences. The following are examples:

| | | | |
|---|---|---|---|
| BBML | Baby food meal | AVML | Asian vegetable meal |
| LFML | Low fat meal | KSML | Kosher meal |
| SPML | Special meal request | VGML | Vegetarian meal |

If no meal code exists for the client's preference, the request code SPML may be input with a remark, as follows:

3SPML2/DIABETIC MEAL-1.1

(Special meals are not available on all flights, and different types of special meals are offered by various carriers.)

---

**SSR Service Codes**

| | |
|---|---|
| WCHR | Wheelchair (Passenger can climb stairs) |
| WCHS | Wheelchair (Passenger can walk to seat) |
| WCHC | Wheelchair (Passenger must be carried) |
| BLND | Assist blind passenger |
| DEAF | Assist deaf passenger |
| NSST | Seat requested in no-smoking section |
| SMST | Seat requested in smoking section |
| UMNR | Assist unaccompanied minor |
| AVIH | Live animal in cargo hold |
| PETC | Pet in cabin compartment |
| RMKS | Service remarks (followed by free text) |
| XBAG | Excess baggage |
| BSCT | Bassinet |
| BIKE | Bicycle |
| BULK | Bulky baggage |
| CBBG | Cabin baggage |
| DIPL | Diplomatic courier |
| EMER | Emergency travel |
| EXST | Extra seat |
| FRAV | First available |
| FRST | First-time airline passenger |
| FRAG | Fragile baggage |
| GPST | Group seat request |
| MASS | Meet and assist |

---

## SSR Remarks

Descriptive text may be included in other SSR entries besides special meal requests. To illustrate, assume a passenger desires to transport a caged bird in the cabin. For this situation, the code PETC may be input with a description as follows:

> 3PETC/CAGED BIRD

The following are additional examples of SSR entries with descriptive text:

> 3SPML3-1.2/LOW POTASSIUM MEAL
> 3AVIH CUSTOMER-OWNED KENNEL
> 3OTHS SURFBOARD IN HOLD

Note the use of the request code OTHS to request other services not covered by the list of official SSR codes.

**Frequent Flyer Numbers**

Members of airline frequent flyer programs, such as American Airlines AAdvantage or United Airlines MileagePlus, receive mileage credits for travel on a participating carrier. These credits can be exchanged for free tickets, class upgrades, and other rewards. The entry code FF is used to input a frequent traveler account number. The carrier code, segment status, account number, and name reference all must be included in the entry.

To illustrate, assume Mr. Arnold Miles, who is the first passenger in name item 1, will travel on a United flight and is a member of Mileage Plus. The passenger's account number is 665042. The following entry would be used to input the account number:

> FFUA66502-1.1

In this example, the status HK indicates that the passenger holds a confirmed reservation on a United flight. The carrier code UA refers to the confirmed flight segment. UA is also typed before the account number to identify the frequent flyer program. A dash is typed before the name reference.

In some cases, a client may receive mileage credits for flying on a different carrier. For instance, passengers who belong to the United Mileage Plus program can receive mileage credits for traveling on British Midland, and passengers who belong to the AAdvantage program can receive credits for traveling on Qantas.

**Child SSR**

The SSR code CHLD is used to advise the airlines of a child passenger, as follows:

> 3CHLD/18APR04-1.4

In this example, the child's date of birth is 18 April, 2004.

## Advanced Passenger Information

Advanced Passenger Information (API) includes passport, visa, and address details, which must be transmitted to the airlines in an international itinerary, to comply with the security and immigration procedures of the applicable countries.

## Passport Details

The request code DOCS is used to input a passenger's passport details, as follows:

3DOCS/P/<Issuing Country>/<Passport Number>/<Nationality>/<Date of Birth>/<Sex>/<Expiry Date>/<Surname>/<Given Name>-<Passenger reference>

**Example:**
3DOCS/P/USA/64248762/USA/12JUL68/M/24SEP12/SMITH/PETER/JOHN-1.1

This example consists of the following information:

| | |
|---|---|
| Service request: | 3 |
| SSR/request code: | DOCS |
| Document type: | /P |
| Issuing country: | /USA |
| Passport number: | /64248762 |
| Nationality: | /USA |
| Date of birth: | /12JUL68 |
| Sex: | /M |
| Expiry date: | /24SEP18 |
| Surname: | /SMITH |
| Given name: | /PETER |
| Passenger association: | -1.1 |

In this entry, the passport number is 64248762, issued in the United States. The passenger's date of birth is 12 July, 1968. The passport expires 24 September 2018. The passport holder is Peter John Smith, who is male.

When an infant travels by means of a parent's passport, the additional modifier /H is typed at the end of the entry, to indicate the holder of the passport.

3/DOCS/P/USA/67247761/USA/18MAR57/F/21JAN20/HILL/MARY/H-1.3

## Visas Details

The request code DOCO is used to input visa details, as follows:

3DOCO/<Place of Birth/<Document Type>/<Place of Issue>/<Date of Issue>/<Country of Validity>-<Passenger reference>

The following is an example:

3DOCO/PARIS FR/V/789789/UK/14JUN14/USA-1.2

This entry indicates that the passenger was born in Paris, France. The document is a visa, number 726382289, issued in Paris on 18 February, 2014. The visa is valid for the USA.

**Passenger Address**

The request code DOCA is used to input the passenger's residential address or destination address. (The destination address is required for all travel to the USA.) The following is an example:

3DOCA/R/USA/6421 N CENTRAL AVE/PHOENIX/AZ/85013-1.1

This entry indicates the passenger's residential address. The secondary code D is input with the destination address, as follows:

3DOCA/D/AUS/HILTON HOTEL/SYDNEY/NSW-1.1

# E-mail Address Field

The entry code P‡ is used to input the client's e-mail address, as follows:

PE‡JOHNKING@ABCSALES.COM‡FR/DREW PIERSON

In this example, ‡FR/ is typed before the sender's name. The following secondary action codes may also be included:

CC          Copy to additional e-mail address
BC          Blind copy
TO           Recipient name

*Examples*

PE‡PHANSON@MUNDCOM.NET‡TO/PETER HANSON
PE‡JANEDOE@NONESUCH.COM‡CC/KCLARK@NONESUCH.COM

Secondary action codes are optional in PE‡ entries and may be omitted. However, a cross (‡) must always be typed after the client's e-mail address, even if no secondary action code is included, as in the following example:

PE‡MDIAZ@ACMETOOLS.COM‡

The entry code 5V‡EM- may be used to insert free-format text in the e-mail message, as follows:

5V‡EM-DEPOSIT REQUIRED 30 DAYS BEFORE ARRIVAL

The following entry is used to end the transaction and send the itinerary to the client's e-mail address:

EM

The e-mail message will contain a link to the Sabre *Virtually There* website, where the client can view the booked itinerary.

# Review

1. What field is used to input free-format text in a PNR?

2. What entry code is used to enter information in the field in question 1?

3. Write the entry to input a reminder to mail the tickets.

4. Write the entry to input the following remark: ARRANGE LIMOUSINE

5. Assume you are making travel arrangements for a client who will purchase his ticket by check. Write the entry to input the form of payment.

6. Write the entry to input the form of payment as an American Express card with the number AX3650513240402212, expiring October 2018.

7. Write the entry to indicate that the ticket will be purchased by cash.

8. What entry code is used to send an OSI message to carriers other than AA?

9. What code is used in an OSI entry to direct the message to all carriers in the itinerary?

10. What entry would be used to send an OSI message to inform British Airways that a passenger is a VIP, the Japanese consul?

11. What entry would be used to send an OSI message to American Airlines to indicate that the passenger is elderly?

12. Write the correct SSR code for each of the following:

    Unaccompanied minor
    Deaf passenger
    Blind passenger
    Wheelchair (passenger can walk up stairs)
    Wheelchair (passenger must be carried)
    Wheelchair (passenger can walk to seat)
    Vegetarian meal
    Kosher meal

13. Assume you are booking flight reservations for a client who is blind. The passenger will travel unaccompanied on a DL flight. What entry would be input to request assistance?

Copyright © 2015, Dennis L. Foster

14. Assume you are creating a PNR for the following clients:

```
1.1FRANKS/CARL    2.2GOLDBERG/JAMES/ETTA MRS
```

Mr. Goldberg requests a vegetarian meal on a JL flight. What entry would be input to request the special meal?

15. Write the entry to input the following agency address: Ticket Express, 8254 Cactus Blvd, Phoenix AZ 85023.

16. Write the entry to input the following client address: Mr T Mathews, 52 Oak Street, Ft. Lauderdale FL 33329.

17. Write the entry to input the following client e-mail address: HCHUNG@GEOSYS.COM

18. What entry is used to end the transaction and send the itinerary to the client's e-mail address?

19. Assume a client is booked on KL. Her passport number is 60755484, issued in the US. The date of birth is 28 April, 1965. The passport expires 12 January, 2020. The passport holder is Kristin Larsen, a female. Write the entry to input the passenger's passport details.

20. Assume a client is booked on a NW flight. The passenger was born in Miami. His visa number is 877365507, issued in Miami on 12 November, 2014. The visa is valid for China. Write the entry to input the passenger's visa details.

46

# Modifying the Itinerary

## Objectives

*After completing this unit, you should be able to do the following:*

1. Retrieve a PNR by passenger name.
2. Retrieve a PNR by flight, departure date, board point, and passenger name.
3. Retrieve a PNR by record locator number.
4. Cancel one or more segments.
5. Cancel and rebook a segment with one entry.
6. Insert a segment in the itinerary.
7. Identify and interpret common status/action codes.
8. Change segment status.

## Retrieving by Surname

The following format is used to retrieve a reservation by surname:

*–<Surname>

**Example:**
*–FROST

Only the surname is required in this entry, but the selection can be narrowed by including the first name or initial. For instance, assume a travel agent previously created a PNR for Mr. Coleridge, who inquires about his flight reservations. The following entry may be used to retrieve the passenger's PNR:

    *–COLERIDGE

The system responds by retrieving the PNR and placing it in the agent's work area. The PNR is displayed as follows:

```
    1.2HUNTER/RICHARD MR/LAUREN MRS
 1 UA  98Y 12OCT 2 SFOATL HK2  1050A  627P /DCUA /E
 2 UA 311Y 17OCT 7 ATLSFO HK2   335P  857P /DCUA /E
 TKT/TIME LIMIT -
    1.TAW11OCT/
 PHONES-
    1.SFO415-342-1661-A
    2.SFO415-451-7823-B
    3.SFO415-745-2003-H
 RECEIVED FROM - MR
 Q0T0*Q0T0.A14 SGTTWE
```

Note in the itinerary that segments 1 and 2 have the status HK. When a segment is sold, the status SS indicates that the reservation will be confirmed when the transaction is ended. When the system accepts an entry to end transact, the segment status SS is changed to HK automatically. The last line shows the office identification code and agent code . The four-character identification code is called the pseudo city. The six character PNR code is called the record locator and is assigned by the system when the transaction is ended.

A PNR can be retrieved by any of the airlines in the itinerary, or by the booking source. Under most circumstances, a travel agency cannot retrieve a PNR that was created by another travel agency or by an airline, unless authorization is obtained from the booking source. However, Sabre users can retrieve PNRs that were booked directly with American Airlines.

Retrieving a PNR created by another booking source is called claiming a reservation. To claim a reservation, authorization must be obtained from the agency that created the PNR. For example, assume a passenger arranged a reservation with Continental Airlines, intending to pick up the tickets at the airport. He later decides to purchase the tickets at an agency near his office. However, the agency is a Sabre subscriber. Before the travel agent can retrieve the client's reservation, the PNR must be released by the airline. In this situation, the agent phones the booking source and requests the PNR to be released to the agency for ticketing.

**Examples of Retrieving by Surname**

*-KLINGINSMITH
*-JOSLYN/J
*-HARCOURT/TMR

**Similar Name Lists**

If multiple PNRs exist for passengers with the same surname, Sabre will display a similar name list showing the names and travel dates of the PNRs. Each record is numbered, as follows:

```
01 WALTERS/ANN MS 04JUN-17JUN   02 WALTERS/ANN MS   04JUN-02JUL
03 WALTERS/T MR    10JUN-12JUN   04 WEAVER/PETER MR 12JUN-18JUN
05 WEBB/KENNETH    02JUN-05JUN   06 WEBSTER/J MRS   10JUN-21JUN
07 WILLIAMS/SAMUE 12JUN-20JUN   08 WILLIAMS/Y MS    08JUN-13JUN
09 WILSON/CARL     12JUL-27JUL   10 WOODALL/M MR     08JUN-22JUN
```

To display the desired record, the following format is used:

    *2

This entry will display item 2 of the similar name list. The list can be redisplayed as follows:

    *L

**Retrieving by Flight, Date, and Surname**

A PNR may also be retrieved by flight, date, and surname, as follows:

*<Carrier><Flight>/<Date>-<Surname>

48

**Example:**
*UA244/1OAUG-THEISSEN

This example will retrieve the PNR for passenger Theissen, who is scheduled to depart on UA 244 on 10 August.

### Retrieving by the Record Locator

When a PNR is stored, Sabre assigns a six-digit code called a record locator. This code may be used to retrieve the PNR from storage as follows:

*<Record Locator>

**Example:**
*STHHYU


# Canceling Segments

Occasionally, an existing reservation may need to be canceled, because the passenger has changed his or her travel plans, or an airline schedule change has occurred. The entry code X is used to cancel a segment, as follows:

X<Segment Number>

**Example:**
X2

Sabre responds as follows:

```
NXT REPLACES 2
```

The next segment that is booked before the itinerary is redisplayed will replace the one just canceled. If the itinerary is redisplayed without booking a new segment, the itinerary will be reordered.

**Example**

Assume a travel agent previously booked a reservation for J. Kirk. The passenger wishes to cancel the outbound flight. The agent first retrieves the PNR, as follows:

    *–KIRK

Assume Sabre displays the PNR. To cancel the first segment, the agent inputs the following entry:

X1

Sabre responds as follows:

`NXT REPLACES 1`

The response indicates that if a new segment is sold, it will replace segment 1. Let's say the passenger does not wish to book a replacement flight at this time. To reorder the remaining segments of the itinerary, the agent redisplays the itinerary as follows:

*I

When a PNR is created or changed, a notation must be made of the person who requested the service. The received-from entry is input as follows:

6P

In this example, the abbreviation "P" is used to indicate that the change was received from the passenger. The store the changes, the agent ends the transaction as follows:

E

## Canceling and Rebooking a Segment

Assume a client was previously booked on a round trip from La Paz to Sao Paulo and now would like to change the return flight. Assuming the return flight is segment 2, the following entry would be used to cancel the flight:

X2

The system responds as follows:

`NXT REPLACES 2`

The next air segment booked will replace the canceled segment (2). After selling the segment, the agent redisplays the itinerary to reorder the segments, inputs the received-from information, and then ends the transaction.

 The cross (‡) can be used to cancel and rebook with one entry. For example, the following entry would be used to cancel segment 3 and rebook 2 seats on AA 202 in Y class on 24 October from DFW to SFO:

X3‡0AA202Y24OCTDFWSFONN2

 If an availability display is present, a segment can be canceled and rebooked with one entry as follows:

X1‡01Y3

50

This example will cancel segment 1 and rebook 1 seat in Y class from line 3 of an availability display.

**Canceling Multiple Segments**

A slash may be used to cancel multiple segments with one entry, as follows:

    X1/3

This example will cancel segments 1 and 3.

A range of consecutive segments may be canceled as follows:

    X1-4

Note that this entry has the same effect as the entry *X1/2/3/4.*

The following entry may be used to cancel the entire itinerary:

    XI

# Changing Segment Status

When a waitlisted segment is confirmed, Sabre changes the segment status from HL (have listed) to KL (confirmed from list). When this situation occurs, the agent must change the segment status to HK before the ticket can be issued. Normally, the agent contacts the passenger to confirm the reservation. If the passenger accepts the confirmed segment, the agent will change the segment status from KL to HK. A dot (.) is used to change segment status, as follows:

.<Segment><Status>

**Example:**
.1HK

This example will change the status of segment 1 to HK.

To illustrate, assume a travel agent previously booked the following reservation:

```
 1.2KEATS/JOHN MR/LORRAINE MRS
 1 DL 296Y 12SEP 1 ORDBOS KL2  815A 1113A /DCDL
 2 DL1448Y 12SEP 1 ORDBOS HK2  620P  917P /DCDL
 3 DL 865Y 15SEP 4 BOSORD HK2  735A  858A /DCDL
```

In this example, the passengers were previously waitlisted on DL 296 departing from O'Hare at 815A and confirmed on DL 1448 departing at 620P.Segment 1 has now cleared the waitlist, as indicated by the status KL. The agent first notifies the client to reconfirm the flight and then changes the segment status to HK, as follows:

.1HK

Each time a PNR is change or updated, a received-from item should be input. Assume the agent notified Mrs. Keats about the status change. The following entry may be used to input the received-from information and end the transaction:

6MRSΣE

---

## Segment Status Codes

| Code | Meaning | Action |
|------|---------|--------|
| HK | Holding confirmed status | No action is required. |
| HL | Holding waitlisted status | No action is required. |
| KK | Confirmed by carrier | Notify the client and change the status to HK. |
| KL | Confirmed from waitlist | Notify the client and change the status to HK. |
| PN | Pending need | No action is required. After 24 hours, change the status to IN to request again. |
| SB | Stand by passenger | No action is required. |
| SC | Schedule change | Notify the client and change the status to HK. |
| UC | Unable to confirm | Cancel the segment and sell an alternative flight. |
| UN | Unable to sell | Cancel the segment and sell an alternative flight. |
| US | Unable to sell | To waitlist, change the status to HL. |
| UU | Unable/unable | To waitlist, change the status to HL. |
| WK | Was confirmed | Cancel the segment and confirm the alternative (SC) segment. |

---

### Handling Status Changes

Some segment status codes do not require any action. However, the following situations require the agent to notify the passenger and change the segment status:

*Confirmed Seat Requests*

If a seat request exceeds the maximum number shown in the seat quota, the segment will have the status NN. When the transaction is ended, a message is transmitted to the carrier requesting the seats. Until a reply is received from the carrier, the segment will have the status HN, NN, or PN.

If the space is confirmed by the carrier, the segment status will be changed to KK. The PNR will be placed in an electronic holding area called the confirmation queue. Each business day, the agent can look in the queue to see which PNRs have itineraries with confirmed seat requests. (You will learn how to work with queues later.)

*Declined Seat Requests*

Occasionally, space requested from a carrier in an NN segment may be declined, either because of a schedule change or because the flight is completely sold out. When a seat request is declined, the segment may have one of the following status codes:

| | |
|------|-------------------|
| UC | Unable to confirm |
| US | Unable to sell |
| UU | Unable/unable |

If the status is UC, the agent must cancel the segment and book an alternative flight. However, if the status is US or UU, the segment can be waitlisted by changing the status to HK. If the client chooses not be waitlisted on the flight, the agent should cancel the segment and book an alternative flight.

As an example, assume an itinerary has the following segment:

```
1 AC 790 20MAY 3 LAXYYZ US5 105P  825P
```

In this example, five seats were requested on an Air Canada flight. However, the carrier was unable to confirm the space, as indicated by the status US. Assume the clients would like to be waitlisted on the flight. The following entry would be used to change the segment status:

.1HL

In this case, an alternative flight should also be booked to protect the passengers.

*Schedule Changes*

When a segment is affected by a schedule change, or if a flight ceases to operate, the segment may have one of the following status codes:

| | |
|------|-------------------------|
| UC | Unable to confirm |
| UN | Unable to sell |
| US | Unable to sell |
| UU | Unable/unable |
| WK | Was confirmed |
| WL | Was waitlisted |
| YK | Cancel confirmed segment |

If a segment has any of the above status codes, the agent must cancel the segment and book an alternative flight.

When a flight is affected by a schedule change, the airline may protect the client by recommending an alternative segment. In this case, the original segment may have the status WK (was confirmed) or WL (was waitlisted). The alternative segment will appear in the itinerary with the status SC (schedule change). When a segment has this status, the agent should notify the client immediately about the schedule change. If the passenger accepts the alternative segment, the agent then would change the segment status from SC to HK to secure the reservation, and cancel the WK or WL segment. If the client declines the alternative segment, the agent would cancel the segment and book a different flight.

To illustrate, assume an itinerary has the following segment:

```
1 AA4243Y 30MAR 5 MKEORD SS1   540A   620A
```

When the transaction is ended, the segment status is changed automatically from SS to HK. If the PNR is then redisplayed, the itinerary will appear as follows:

```
1 AA4243Y 30MAR 5 MKEORD HK1   540A   620A
```

Now let us assume that, before the departure date a schedule change occurs and AA 4243 no longer operates on Friday. When the PNR is retrieved and the itinerary displayed, the segment appears as follows:

```
1 AA4243Y 30MAR 5 MKEORD WK1   540A   620A
2 AA4224Y 30MAR 5 MKEORD SC1   734A   814A
```

The segment status WK indicates that AA 4243 will not operate. However, the client has been protected on AA 4224, as indicated by the status SC in segment 2. Assume the client accepts the alternative flight. The agent secures the reservation by changing the segment status from SC to HK, as follows:

```
.2HK
```

The following entry would be used to cancel the WK segment:

```
X1
```

The itinerary now appears as follows:

```
1 AA4224Y 30MAR 5 MKEORD HK1   734A   814A
```

# Review

1. Write the correct entry to retrieve the PNR for passenger Templeton.

2. Assume you previously booked flight reservations for passenger Greene. Write the entry to retrieve the client's PNR.

3. Write the correct entry to retrieve the PNR for passenger Norman.

4. Passenger Kleinman will depart on AA 2784 on 18 June. Write the correct entry to retrieve the PNR by flight, date, and name.

5. Write the entry to retrieve the PNR for the record locator SWKLQH.

6. Write the correct entry to display all fields of a PNR, including the itinerary.

7. Which entry will display only the itinerary?

8. Which entry will display only the passenger data fields?

9. What entry code is used to cancel an air segment?

10. What entry would cancel the third segment of an itinerary?

11. Assume two clients are waitlisted on a flight in segment 1 and confirmed in segment 2. The waitlisted flight fails to clear the waitlist. Write the correct entry to cancel the waitlisted segment.

12. Which entry would cancel the waitlisted segment in question 11 and rebook the same flight and class on 15 June?

13. Which entry would be used to cancel segments 1, 3, and 7?

14. What entry would cancel the entire itinerary?

15. What key is used to insert a new segment in an itinerary?

16. Write the entry to insert after segment 2.

17. Write the entry to insert an ARNK segment after segment 5.

18. Write the correct entry to insert after segment 3 and sell 2 seats in B class on DL 119 on 19 January from CDG to JFK.

19. Write the entry to insert after segment 1 and sell 2 seats in Y class on the flight in line 5 of an availability display.

20. Write the entry to change the status of segment 4 to HK.

# Editing a PNR

## Objectives

*After completing this unit, you should be able to do the following:*

1. Delete passenger data in a PNR.
2. Change passenger data.
3. Reduce the number in the party.
4. Divide passengers from a PNR.

## Deleting Passenger Data

Information stored in the passenger data field of an existing PNR can be deleted or changed while the PNR is in the agent work area. The change code (¤) may be used for this purpose. The following format is used to delete a data item:

<Field Identifier><Item Number>¤

## Example:
–2¤

The entry above would delete the second name item from a displayed PNR. If the specified field has only one data item, the item number 1 may be omitted, as in the following example:

    7¤

This entry would be used to delete the ticketing item, in a PNR with one item in the ticketing field. If a name item consists of multiple passengers, name reference may be used to delete a passenger within the name item. For example, assume a PNR has the following name field:

        1.2HICKORY/NEAL MR/MARY MRS   2.2DICKORY/KEVIN MR/EVE MRS

Assume Mrs. Y. Dickory, the second passenger in name item 2, has decided not to travel. The following entry may be used to delete the passenger name:

            2.2¤

This example will delete only the second passenger in name item 2, but will not affect any other passengers in the name item.

## Examples of Deleting Data Items

92¤     Delete second phone item
–¤      Delete name item in a PNR with one surname
55¤     Delete fifth line of remarks field

**Changing Passenger Data**

To change the information in a passenger data field, the new data is typed after the change code ¤, as follows:

<Field Identifier><Item Number>¤<New data>

**Example:**
−1¤JOHNSON/HOWARD MR

The example above would change the first name item in a displayed PNR. Let us examine some typical situations requiring changes to the passenger data fields. Assume a PNR has the following name items:

```
1.2HOFFMAN/GERARD MR/ANNE MRS   2.2CARLISLE/MARK MR/KAREN MRS
```

Let's say that the second surname is misspelled and the correct spelling is Carlysle. The following entry would be used to change the name item:

```
−2¤2CARLYSLE/MARK MR/KAREN MRS
```

If the PNR has only one name item, the item number 1 may be omitted, as in following example:

```
−¤SANDERS/CHARLES MR
```

To change only the first name or initial in a name item, include the name reference. For example, assume a PNR has the following name item:

```
1.1MORRIS/PAUL MR/SARAH MRS/JOAN MISS
```

Let's say that the third passenger in the name item is Ms. Joanne Morris. In this case, the given name was input incorrectly. The following entry may be used to correct the name item:

```
−1.3¤JOANNE MS
```

The name reference 1.3 indicates the third passenger in name item 1. When a name reference is input to change the first name or initial, the surname must be omitted.

Besides names, other information in the name field can also be added or changed. For example, assume a PNR has the following name field:

```
1.1PULLMAN/THOMAS MR   2.1FRANKS/JOHN MR
```

The following entry would be used to add Mr. Pullman's AAdvantage account number to the name field:

```
−1¤7765443
```

**Examples of Changing Data Items**

| | |
|---|---|
| 92¤602-643-3499-B | Change phone item 2 |
| 52¤-CK | Change second line of remarks field |
| 7¤TAW18JUL/ | Change ticketing field |
| —3¤2LEE/KEITH MR/ANN MRS | Change surname in name item 3 |
| —2.2¤ELAINE MRS | Change specified given name and title |

# Reducing the Number in the Party

No matter how many travelers are booked in a PNR, the number of passengers in the name field must be equal to the number of seats in the itinerary. The following entry format is used to reduce the number in a party:

,<New number>

**Example:**
,2

The example above would reduce the number of passengers to two. When this entry is input, Sabre will change the number of seats in each air segment. However, the name field and any other passenger data fields that are affected by the action must also be changed.

Sabre responds as follows:

```
PARTY NOW 2 STARTING AT 1 NO ACT ON AUX
```

The response indicates that the party now consists of two passengers, starting at segment 1. No action has been taken on any auxiliary segments such as car or hotel segments.

This format can only be used to reduce, but not increase, the number of seats in an itinerary. To increase the number of seats, the agent must cancel and rebook the itinerary.

When a party is reduced, the applicable passenger(s) must be deleted from the name field, so that the number of names is the same as the number of seats booked in the itinerary. Any data items associated with a deleted passenger, such as a home phone or SSR entry, should also be deleted.

# Dividing a PNR

If a PNR has multiple passengers and one or more travelers wish to change their itinerary, the PNR can be divided. When a PNR is divided, a separate record is created for the passengers whose travel plans have changed.

The entry code D is used to divide a PNR that has been retrieved from storage and is in the agent's work area, as follows:

D<Name item>

**Example:**
D2

The example above will divide the passengers in name item 2 from the PNR and create a new record for them. The new PNR will be displayed automatically. The entry code F is then used to file the new PNR.

The following steps are required to divide a PNR:

1. Retrieve the existing PNR.

2. Divide the passengers who want to change their itinerary. A new PNR will be created automatically.

3. Input the received-from item and file the record to save the new PNR. The original PNR will be displayed automatically.

4. Input the received-from item and end the transaction to save the changes in the original PNR.

When a party is divided, Sabre creates a new PNR for the specified passengers. To save the new PNR, the following entry is input:

F

When the new record is filed, the original PNR is redisplayed automatically. Before the PNRs are stored, an OSI item may be input to cross-reference the records, as follows:

3OSI  AA TCP2 W/MORELLI AA336B12JUNORDMIA

The letters "TCP" mean "to complete a party." This entry indicates the passenger will complete a party of 2 with passenger Morelli. They will travel together on AA 336 in B class on 12 June from ORD to MIA.

**Dividing by Name Reference**

To divide a selected passenger within a name item, include the name reference, as follows:

D2.3

This example will divide out third passenger in name item 2, but will have no affect on other passengers within the name item.

To illustrate, assume a PNR contains the following name item:

1.3LEONARD/JOHN MR/RHONDA MRS/C MSTR

Let's say that Mrs. Leonard would like to change her itinerary. The following entry may be used to divide the PNR:

60

D1.2

The name reference 1.2 indicates the second passenger in name item 1.

**Dividing Multiple Passengers**

To divide multiple passengers, type an asterisk (*) to separate the names. For example, to divide the passengers in name items 1 and 3, the following entry may be used:

D1*3

Name reference may also be included in this entry. To illustrate, assume a PNR contains the following name field:

```
1.2GUERRERA/JUAN MR/SUSAN MRS   2.2LOPEZ/HECTOR MR/LISA MRS
```

Assume that Susan Guerrera and Lisa Lopez decide to change their itinerary. The following entry may be used to divide the PNR:

D1.2*2.2

# Review

1. What entry code is used to reduce the number of passengers in a PNR?

2. Write the correct entry to reduce the party to one passenger.

3. Assume a PNR has the following name field:

    ```
    1.1BRADLEY/FRANK    2.1SIMON/ANDREW    3.1PARKER/THOMAS
    ```

Mr. Simon decides not to travel. Write the correct entry to reduce the party.

4. What entry will delete only Mr. Simon from the name field in question 15?

5. Assume a PNR has the following name field:

    ```
    1.2GREENE/CHARLES MR/EDNA MRS
    ```

If Edna Greene decides not to travel, what entry would be used to reduce the party?

6. What code is used to divide a passenger from the PNR?

7. What code is used to file a new PNR created by dividing a party?

8. Assume a PNR has the following name field:

    ```
    1.1MERITT/RAYMOND MR    2.1GOULD/FRANCINE MS
    ```

What entry would divide Ms. Gould from the PNR?

9. Assume a client will travel with passenger Thomas on BA 742 in M class on 18 June from LHR to HKG. Write the correct entry to cross-reference the PNRs.

10. Assume a PNR has the following names:

    ```
    1.2MUELLER/HENRY MR/GERTRUDE MRS    2.2STEIN/JASON MR/ANNE MRS
    ```

Write the correct entry to divide Henry Mueller and Jason Stein.

# Fare Displays

## Objectives

*After completing this unit, you should be able to do the following:*

1. Display fares by city pair, date, and carrier.
2. Interpret the fare display.
3. Obtain a display of the lowest fares offered by all carriers.
4. Interpret the fare display.
5. Obtain a fare display for a selected fare type.
6. Modify a fare display.
7. Display fare rules pertaining to a given fare basis.

The fare level is indicated by the class of service. On major airlines, the two basic classes are premium or first class and economy or coach class. Premium (P) or first (F) class is the most expensive class of service. Economy or coach (Y) class may also be called standard class. Many carriers offer a premium coach (C or J) class that is less expensive than first class but more expensive than coach. Depending on the carrier, this class of service may be called business, club, connoisseur, or ambassador class, etc.

## Fare Basis

A fare basis is a price category determined by the class of service and factors such as the destination, season, day of the week, one-way or round trip travel, advance purchase, or the length of the stay. Each fare basis has a primary code and one or more secondary codes.

For instance, the YLE30 fare basis applies to travel in the economy cabin during the low season. The fare is an excursion fare, and the maximum stay is 30 days. The primary code Y indicates the economy cabin, the secondary code L indicates the low season, and E indicates an excursion (restricted round-trip) fare. The digits indicate the maximum stay.

## Fare Rules

Discount fares, sometimes called restricted or inventory fares, are offered by various carriers. Passengers who travel at a discount fare receive the same level of service as other coach passengers, but the fares have various restrictions.

For example, the ticket must be purchased a preset number of days before departure, and the itinerary must originate and terminate at the same point. Often, the outbound and return segments must be booked on the same carrier. Other restrictions, such as a minimum stay, a Saturday stayover, and penalties for cancellation or changes, may also apply.

## Displaying a Fare Quote

A fare quote is a display of fares for a specified carrier, listed from most expensive to least expensive. The entry code FQ is used to obtain a fare quote, as follows:

FQ<City pair><Departure date>

**Example:**
FQDFWSEA18MAR

This example will display a fare quote for travel from Dallas-Ft. Worth to Seattle on 18 March. Normal and excursion fares for all carriers will be displayed. If the date is omitted, fares will be displayed for the current date.

The fare quote is displayed as follows:

```
DFW-SEA        SHOP           MON 18MAR                          USD
    TAXES/FEES/US PFC - NOT INCL IN TOTAL
**     DFWSEA.WH      18MAR                       MPM 2287
       FARE BASIS    BK        FARE    CX    TRAVEL-TICKET AP    MINMAX
  1    WXLPNO        W R      292.00   US       ----        -/‡  ‡‡/ 1M
  2    QXE21         Q R      320.00   AA       ----        -/‡  ‡‡/ 1M
  3    VA21N         V R      334.00   UA       ----        -/‡  ‡‡/ 2M
  4    HLPXSU        H R      342.00   CO       ----        -/‡  ‡‡/ 3M
  5    QLE21N        Q R      344.00   DL       ----        -/‡  ‡‡/ 6M
  6    BLXP50        B R      485.00   US       ----        -/‡  ‡‡/ 6M
  7    LXE21         L R      492.00   AA       ----        -/‡  ‡‡/ 3M
```

The line number can be used to display the fare rules. The fare basis and booking code (BK) are shown for each fare. For example, the fare in line 6 has the fare basis BLXP50, and the booking code B would be used to sell a segment at this fare. The code on the right of the booking code is called the fare application. R indicates a round-trip fare, and X indicates a one-way fare.

The carrier is shown in the CX column. The fare in line 1 is valid for travel on US. If a travel date or ticket date applies, the dates are shown in the TRAVEL-TICKET column.

The following information may appear in the TRAVEL-TICKET column:

| | | |
|---|---|---|
| S12MY | S | First date on which the fare may be sold |
| E24JN | E | Effective date for outbound travel |
| D30AP | D | Discontinue date for outbound travel |
| C01JL | C | Date on which travel must be completed |
| R12MY | R | Date on which return travel must commence |
| T30NOV | T | Last ticket date |
| S*GA | | Subject to government approval |
| ----- | | No travel/ticket restrictions apply |

If a fare has an advance purchase requirement, the number of days is given in the AP column. If a minimum or maximum stay is required, the information is shown in the MIN/MAX column. The code ‡‡ signifies that the agent must consult the fare rules to determine the requirement.

A specific carrier may be requested as follows:

FQLAXAKL22AUG−NZ

The return date may be specified as follows:

FQJFKLHR24APR‡R28APR

## Fare Quote Options

The secondary code ‡B may be used to specify a booking code or class, as follows:

FQLONATL29APR−DL‡BM

The example above requests fare in M class for travel on Delta.
One-way or round-trip fares may be requested as follows:

| | |
|---|---|
| FQLAXNRT18MAR‡OW | One-way fares |
| FQLAXNRT18MAR‡RT | Round-trip fares |

The secondary code ‡VN may be used to display fares without date validation, as follows:

FQNYCLON26JUN‡VN

### Modifying a Fare Quote Display

When a fare quote is displayed, the entry code FQ* can be used to modify the date, fare type, or carrier. For example, the following entry will change the departure date to 24 June:

FQ*24JUN

This entry will display fares for the same city pair and carrier as in the existing display, based on the new departure date.
The carrier may be changed as follows:

FQ*−DL

This example will change the display to show Delta fares for the same city pair and date.

### Scrolling the Display

The following entries may be used to scroll the display:

| | |
|---|---|
| MD | Move down |
| MU | Move up |
| MT | Move to the top |
| MB | Move to the bottom |

The top of the display is the first character of the first line. The bottom of the display is the last character of the last line. The first header line shows the city pair, departure date, and currency. The next two lines show the number of nonstop, direct, and connecting flights operated by each carrier.

**Displaying a Fare Quote from Availability**

The entry code FQL can be used to obtain a fare quote from a city pair availability display, as follows:

FQL3

This entry will display a fare quote for the carrier in the selected line of the availability display.

# Total Access Fare Displays

The Total Access function can be used to obtain a fare display from the reservation system of a participating carrier. Total Access fares may be displayed as follows:

FQLAXSFO12JUNNLX¤UA

This entry will link with the United reservation system and display fares for travel from Los Angeles to San Francisco on 12 June. The fare type code NLX is used to display normal and excursion fares. Note that . is typed before the carrier code.

When this entry is input, SABRE responds as follows:

```
NORMAL/EXCURSION FARES
           USD      FARE           MIN/  CNL  TRVL DATES   TKT DATES
    CX     FARE     BASIS      AP   MAX  FEE  FIRST/LAST   FIRST/LAST
  1 UA    189.00R   HE21NR     21  SU/30 NR     -/-          -/-
  2 UA    189.00R   VE21       21  SU/30 NR     -/-          -/-
  3 UA    202.00R   VE14NR     14  SU/30 NR     -/-          -/-
  4 UA    202.00R   QE7NR       7  SU/30 NR     -/-          -/-
  5 UA    202.00R   QE14NR     14  SU/30 NR     -/-          -/-
  6 UA    202.00R   BE14M      14  SU/60 NR     -/-          -/-
```

Total Access fares are displayed in the host's format. This United display shows the carrier, fare, fare basis, and a summary of applicable rules.

# Fare Rules

The booking code, valid dates, and restrictions that pertain to a particular fare basis are set forth in the fare rules. When a fare quote is displayed, the entry code RD may be used to obtain a rules display, as follows:

> RD5

The example above will display the rules for the fare basis in line 5 of a displayed fare quote.

## Fare Rule Categories

The categories in a rules display may vary, depending on the fare basis and carrier. However, the same item number and heading is used for each category. Any of the following categories may appear in a rules display:

| | |
|---|---|
| 00 RULE APPL | Rule application |
| 01 ELIGIBILITY | Fare eligibility |
| 02 DAY/TIME | Day/time restrictions |
| 03 SEASON | Season for which fare is valid |
| 04 FLIGHT APPL | Flight application |
| 05 ADV RES/TKT | Advance reservation and ticketing |
| 06 MIN STAY | Minimum stay requirements |
| 07 MAX STAY | Maximum stay requirements |
| 08 STOPOVERS | Permitted stopovers |
| 09 TRANSFERS | Permitted transfers |
| 10 COMBINATIONS | Rules governing combined fares |
| 11 BLACKOUTS | Blackout dates |
| 12 SURCHARGES | Surcharges which may be applied |
| 13 ACCOMP TRAVEL | Accompanied travel |
| 14 TRAVEL RESTR | Travel restrictions |
| 15 SALES RESTR | Sales restrictions |
| 16 PENALTIES | Penalties for canceling or changing |
| 17 HIP/MILEAGE | Higher intermediate points and mileage restrictions |
| 18 TICKET ENDO | Ticket endorsement |
| 19 CHILDREN DISC | Discounts for children of a specified age |
| 20 TOUR COND DISC | Tour conductor discounts |
| 21 AGENT DISC | Agent discounts |
| 22 ALL OTHER DISC | All other discounts |
| 23 MISC PROVISIONS | Miscellaneous restrictions |

## Displaying a Rules Menu

The secondary code *M can be used to display a menu of rule categories. When the menu is displayed, categories can be selected by item number.

> RD2*M

Each category in the rules menu has an item number. The entry code RD* is to display a category from the menu. For example, assume you want to check the effective and expiration dates. The following entry may be used to display the category:

RD*9

In the rules menu, the category pertaining to effective and expiration dates is item 9.

One or more categories may apply to a particular fare basis. However, same item number is used for each category, no matter how many categories are displayed.

**Displaying Fare Rules without a Fare Quote**

The following format is used to display fare rules without a fare quote display:

RD<City pair><Departure date><Fare basis>-<Carrier>

**Example:**
RDSFOBOS10MAYQAP7-UA

The example above will display the rules for the QAP7 fare basis for travel on UA, departing from SFO to BOS on 10 May.

The secondary code *M can be used to display the rules menu, as follows:

RDORDSEA22JUNVLE70NR-DL*M

This example will display the menu of fare rules for the VLE70NR fare basis for travel on Delta from ORD to SEA on 22 June.

# Review

Write the correct entry to do each of the following:

1. Display fares for travel on United from Paris (PAR) to Denver (DEN) on 17 August.

2. Display fares for OA for travel on 23 March from London (LON) to Athens (ATH).

3. Display round-trip fares for travel on BA on 28 January from London (LON) to Hong Kong (HKG).

4. Change the date of an existing fare display to 19 June.

5. Change the carrier to Delta.

6. Display fares for the carrier in line 4 of a city pair availability display.

7. Display fares for travel from Los Angeles (LAX) to Perth (PER) on 24 March, for return on 2 April.

8. Display the rules for the fare basis in line 2 of a fare quote display.

9. Display the menu of fare rules for the fare basis in line 6.

10. Display paragraph 5 from the rules menu.

11. Display the rules for the HLE21N fare basis for travel on UA from Denver (DEN) to Seattle (SEA) on 31 July.

# Itinerary Pricing

## Objectives

*After completing this unit, you should be able to do the following:*

1. Price a booked itinerary.
2. Identify common passenger type codes.
3. Price an itinerary using passenger type codes.
4. Price an itinerary with name selection.
5. Price an itinerary with segment selection.
6. Price an itinerary at the lowest available fare regardless of the class booked.

The itinerary pricing function is used to determine the total fare for an air itinerary. When Sabre prices an itinerary, it takes into consideration any applicable fare rules and joint fare applications.

The following entry will price an itinerary for all passengers and segments at the class of service booked:

WP

Sabre responds as follows:

```
WP
         BASE FARE                      TAXES              TOTAL
  1-    USD2246.30                    183.47XT         USD2429.77ADT
    XT    168.47US       9.00ZP         6.00XF
          2246.30                      183.47             2429.77TTL
ADT-01   YUA Y26
 SFO UA ATL925.00YUA AA MIA409.26Y26 AA SFO Q1.85 910.19Y26
 2246.30 END ZPSFO2.25ATL2.25MIA2.25DFW2.25 XFATL3MIA3
```

The price response shows the number of passengers that have been priced, followed by the base fare, taxes, and total fare for each passenger. In this example, the base fare for each passenger is 2246.00 and the total fare, including taxes, is 2429.77.

## Pricing with Passenger Type Codes

When the basic pricing entry is input, Sabre uses the passenger type codes in the name field to price the itinerary. Occasionally, it may be necessary to specify a different passenger type. For instance, a travel agent may want to obtain a discount fare for military personnel or senior citizens (elderly passengers) although they were originally booked as normal adults. Special fares for such passengers may be requested by means of a passenger type code (PTC).

The following PTCs are used in itinerary pricing entries:

| | |
|---|---|
| ADT | Adult |
| ASB | Adult stand-by |
| CHD | Child |
| C09 | Child (including age) |
| CMP | Companion |
| CLG | Clergy |
| CSB | Clergy Stand-by |
| CVN | Convention |
| FFY | Frequent flyer |
| FDT | Family plan adult |
| ACC | Family plan accompanying adult |
| F10 | Family plan child (including age) |
| GTR | Government transportation |
| GCF | Government contract |
| INF | Infant |
| MDP | Military dependent |
| MIL | Military |
| MLD | Military stationed in U.S. |
| SCB | Senior citizen stand-by |
| SRC | Senior citizen |
| STU | Student |
| ITB | Individual inclusive tour basing |
| ITC | Child's tour basing |
| YSB | Youth Stand-by |
| YTH | Youth |
| ARP | Association of Retired Persons |

Itineraries cannot be priced for every PTC.

When a PTC is input in a pricing entry, Sabre calculates the price based on the appropriate fare type. For example, if C08 is input, the itinerary will be priced using child fares applicable to a child of age 8, if available.

To specify a passenger type, the secondary code P must be typed before the PTC, as follows:

WPPSRC

This example requests a price based on senior citizen fares.

To price a party using both adult and child fares or infant fares, the appropriate PTC must be input for each member of the party. For example, to price two passengers using adult fares and one passenger using child fares applicable to a child of age 10, the following entry would be used:

WPP2ADT/C10

**Segment Selection**

The secondary code S may be used to price only selected segments, as follows:

WPS3/5

The example above will price only segments 3 and 5. No other segments will be priced.

**Pricing with Name Selection**

The secondary code N may be used to price only selected passengers, as follows:

WPN1.4

The example above will price only the fourth passenger in the first name item. To illustrate, assume a PNR has the following passenger names:

```
1.2KNUTZ/RONALD MR/LOIS MRS    2.2BOLTZ/EDWARD MR/FIONA MRS
```

Let's say Mrs. Boltz requests the price of her ticket only. The following entry may be used to obtain a price for the selected passenger:

WPN2.2

Now assume the client requests the price for both Mrs. Knutz and Mrs. Boltz. The following entry may be used to price the itinerary for the selected passengers:

WPN1.2/2.2

**Forcing a Connection**

When an itinerary includes a valid connection with a connecting time of four hours or less, the itinerary is priced based on the throughfare. However, in rare instances, a connection has connecting time of more than four hours. In this case, Sabre will price each leg of the connection as a separate flight. To force Sabre to use a throughfare, the secondary code X may be used, as follows:

WPX2

In this example, segment 2 will be priced as a connecting flight.

**Specifying a Future Ticketing Date**

A future ticketing date may be specified in a pricing entry to take advantage of an anticipated fare change. The secondary code B is used to indicate a future ticketing date, as follows:

WPB18SEP

In this example, the itinerary will be priced based on a ticketing date of 18 September.

**Specifying a Fare Basis**

The secondary code Q is used to specify a fare basis, as follows:

WPQVAP21

The example above will price a displayed itinerary using the VAP21 fare basis.

Specific segments can be priced using different fare basis codes. For instance, the following entry will price segment 1 at the ME70 fare basis and price segment 2 at the KAP7 fare basis:

WPS1*QME70.S2*QKAP7

Observe that a cross (.) is typed to separate the first segment and fare basis from the second segment and fare basis. The secondary code Q is typed before each fare basis.

Pricing an itinerary at a specifed fare basis is referred to as command pricing or phase 3.5 pricing.

## Bargain Finder Entries

The following entry may be used to price an itinerary at the lowest available fare:

WPNC

When this entry is used, Sabre searches for the lowest applicable fare for each segment booked. The price is displayed as follows:

```
WPNC
12OCT DEPARTURE DATE-----LAST DAY TO PURCHASE   4AUG
        BASE FARE                   TAXES              TOTAL
 1-   USD1815.75                   151.18XT       USD1966.93ADT
    XT     136.18US      9.00ZP      6.00XF
           1815.75                  151.18           1966.93TTL
ADT-01   BUA MA14SPN Y26
 SFO UA ATL832.41BUA AA MIA71.30MA14SPN AA SFO Q1.85 910.19Y
 26 1815.75 END ZPSFO2.25ATL2.25MIA2.25DFW2.25 XFATL3MIA3
NO REFUND/CHG FEE USD 75 PLUS FARE DIFF
CHANGE BOOKING CLASS -   1B 2M
```

In this case, a lower fare was located for both segments, based on the VAP14 fare basis. At the bottom of the display, Sabre indicates the segments to rebook and the booking code to use for each segment. In this example, segments 1 and 2 should be changed to Q class to obtain the lowest available fare for each segment.

### Pricing and Rebooking at the Lowest Fare

The following entry will both price and rebook the itinerary at the lowest applicable fare:

WPNCB

Bargain finder entries may be used with name or segment selection codes, as in the following examples:

WPNCB‡S1/3       Price and rebook segments 1 and 3
WPNCB‡N1.1/1.2   Price and rebook name items 1.1 and 1.2

**Bargain Finder Plus**

The following may be used to search for lower fares based on similar itineraries:

> WPNI

When this entry is input, Sabre will search for up to four lower fares, using alternative flight segments to and from the airports in the booked itinerary. The itinerary must consist of no more than six segments. This function is referred to as Bargain Finder Plus.

   After a Bargain Finder Plus response has been obtained, the following entries may be used to rebook the itinerary:

| | |
|---|---|
| WC‡1 | Sell option 1 from Bargain Finder Plus response |
| WC‡2X | Sell option 2 and cancel existing itinerary |

# Stored Pricing

The following entry is used to store the price quote in the PNR:

> PQ

A stored price is not necessarily guaranteed. The actual price at the time of ticketing may be different. The qualifier RQ may be used in a pricing entry to price the itinerary and store the price with one entry, as follows:

> WPRQ

   The following entry is used to display the stored price quote:

> *PQ

   The PQ record is displayed as follows:

```
              PRICE QUOTE RECORD - DETAILS

FARE NOT GUARANTEED UNTIL TICKETED

PQ 1 PADT‡ASA‡RQ

        BASE FARE                 TAXES           TOTAL
     ZAR2520.00                   969.00XT      ZAR3489.00ADT
     XT        22.00EV    172.00ZA  353.00VT      422.00YR
ADT-01 Y YRT Y
 JNB SA DUR134.58.00SA JNB134.58 NUC269.16END ROE7.05890
01 O JNB SA   535Y  12NOV   800A  Y                  12NOV20K
02 O DUR SA   538Y  15NOV   840A  Y                  15JUN20K
    JNB
VALIDATING CARRIER-ZA
Q0X0 JCV  *ATA 1014/10NOV                        PRICE-SYS
```

To delete all PQ records in a PNR, the following entry may be used:

    PQD-ALL

# Review

1. Write the entry to price an entire itinerary.

2. Write the entry to price segments 1, 3, and 5 only.

3. Write the entry to price an itinerary using a throughfare for a connection occurring at segment 5.

4. Write the entry to price an itinerary at the lowest available fare, regardless of the class booked.

5. Write the entry to both price and rebook the itinerary at the lowest applicable fare.

6. Write the entry to price segment 4 only.

7. Assume a PNR has the following names:

       1.3PRINCE/GEORGE MR/HELEN MRS/A MISS

   (a) What entry will price the itinerary just for Mrs. H. Prince.

   (b) What entry will price the itinerary using adult fares for Mr. G. Prince and Mrs. H. Prince, while using child fares for Miss A. Prince, who is 8 years of age?

8. What entry code is used to store pricing instructions for ticketing?

9. Write the entry to store pricing instructions, with UA as the issuing carrier and a 9-percent commission.

10. What entry would price an itinerary using the VA21N fare basis?

# Ticket Issuance

## Objectives

*After completing this unit, you should be able to do the following:*

1. Issue tickets from a retrieved PNR.
2. Specify the issuing carrier.
3. Specify or override the form of payment.
4. Ticket selected passengers and/or segments in a PNR.
5. Indicate a commission.

SABRE can issue tickets for most flight reservations. If any additions or revisions are required, the PNR must be modified and the transaction must be ended before the ticket is issued. If the form of payment was not stored previously, it must be input when tickets are issued.

If the form of payment is stored, the following entry may be used to generate tickets from a retrieved PNR:

W‡

When this entry is input, the name of the carrier in the first segment of the itinerary will be printed in the "issued by" box. The form of payment stored in PNR will be printed in the "form of payment" box.

## Specifying the Issuing Carrier

The issuing carrier is the airline used to validate the ticket. A machine ticket is automatically validated with the issuing carrier's name and IATA code, which are printed in the issued by box on the ticket. Normally, the issuing carrier is the carrier in the first segment of the itinerary. However, in some cases, the agent must override the default carrier and specify a different issuing airline.

The secondary code A is used to specify the issuing carrier, as follows:

W‡ADL

In this example, Delta is the issuing carrier.

## Other Ticket Modifiers

The following modifiers may be used for the form of payment, passenger selection, and segment selection:

| | |
|---|---|
| F<Text> | Form of payment |
| N<Name Item> | Name selection |
| S<Segments> | Segment selection |

## Specifying the form of Payment

If the form of payment is not stored in the PNR, or if the tickets will be purchase by a different form of payment than the one stored, the applicable information may be included in the ticketing entry. To illustrate, assume a travel agent has retrieved a PNR for ticketing. No form of payment exists. The passenger will purchase the tickets by check, and the issuing carrier is NW. The following entry must be used to issue the ticket:

W‡FCK‡ANW

The optional information may be input in any order.

The following are examples of ticketing entries in which the form of payment is included:

| | |
|---|---|
| W‡KP5‡FCK | Check |
| W‡KP5‡FCASH | Cash |
| W‡KP5‡F*AX6023982310920022/1118 | Credit card |

(If the correct form of payment was stored previously, it does not have to be input in the ticketing entry.) If the issuing carrier will be one other than the carrier in the first segment of the itinerary, the carrier must be input.

## Other Secondary Codes

The secondary code ED is used to input information to print in the endorsements/restrictions box, as follows:

W‡EDNONREFUNDABLE

This example will issue tickets and print NONREFUNDABLE in the endorsements/restrictions box.

The secondary code Q may be used to specify a fare basis, as follows:

W‡QVAP21

The example above will issue tickets, using the VAP21 fare basis to price the itinerary.

The secondary code ET is used for exchange tickets. The data is input as follows:

W‡ET017794576541/123/29MAY15SFO

This entry consists of the following information:

| | |
|---|---|
| Ticket entry/exchange ticket: | W‡ET |
| Ticket number: | 00179456541 |
| Ticket coupon number(s): | /123 |
| Ticket issue date and city: | /29MAY15SFO |

The ticket exchange information will be printed in the issued in exchange for box.
The following secondary codes can be used in a ticket entry:

| | |
|---|---|
| P | Passenger Type |
| S | Segment Selection |
| X | Forced Connection |
| N | Name Selection |
| A | Validating Airline |
| KP | Commission Percentage |
| K | Commission Amount |
| U | Tour Number |
| ED | Endorsement Information |
| ET | Exchange Ticket Information |
| F | Form of Payment |
| TE | Tax Exempt Override |
| EX | Excursion Ticketing on Open Segments |
| E | Print Equivalent Amount Paid |
| V | Valid Dates |

## Name Selection

Name selection may be included to ticket only a portion of the party. As an example, assume a PNR has the following Name Field:

        1.3CARLSON/GREGORY MR/TERESA MRS/L MSTR

Let's say you wish to ticket only Mrs. Teresa Carlson and Mstr. L. Carlson at this time. The validating carrier is NW. If the form of payment is stored in the PNR, the following entry may be used to issue the tickets:

        W‡N1.2/1.3‡ANW

## Segment Selection

Segment selection may be included to ticket only a portion of the itinerary. For example, the following entry will ticket only segments 2 and 5 for all passengers in the PNR:

        W‡S2/5‡ADL

**Agency Commissions**

A foreign itinerary may qualify for an agency commission. If a commission applies, the option code KP may be used to indicate the percentage, as follows:

W‡AAF‡KP5

In this example, the issuing carrier is Air France and the commission rate is 5 percent. An exact amount, rather than a percentage, may be indicated as follows:

W‡ABA‡K20.00

In this example, the issuing carrier is BA and the commission amount is 20.00.

**Requesting an E-Ticket**

If e-ticketing is not the default ticketing method, the secondary action code ‡ETR may be used to request an e-ticket, as follows:

W‡ETR

This entry will end the transaction and send the e-ticket request to the airline. If all conditions are met, the e-ticket will be raised in the airline's system.

```
                    ELECTRONIC TICKET
                PASSENGER ITINERARY/RECEIPT

   NAME: MCDONALD/ALLEN MR
                              ETKT NBR: 016 9009918202 0


ISSUING AIRLINE: UNITED AIRLINES
ISSUING AGENT: MY TRAVEL AGENCY ANYTOWN US /U3U8AAA
DATE OF ISSUE: 08JUL


BOOKING REFERENCE: CWHTRE           BOOKING AGENT: U3U8AAA



DATE  AIRLINE           FLT    CLASS     FARE BASIS    STATUS
--------------------------------------------------------------------
12JUL UNITED AIRLINES    548   COACH     YUA           CONFIRMED
        LV: FORT LAUDERDALE    AT:  9:30A
        AR: CHICAGO O'HARE     AT: 11:30A

15JUL UNITED AIRLINES    224   COACH     YUA           CONFIRMED
        LV: CHICAGO O'HARE     AT:  2:25P
        AR: FORT LAUDERDALE    AT:  6:05P

ENDORSEMENTS: VALID ON UA ONLY

FARE CALC: FLL UA CHI 172.10UA FLL 172.10USD344.20END

FORM OF PAYMENT: CHECK
FARE:  USD344.20       TAX: 25.80 US    TAX: 20.40
TOTAL: USD390.40

POSITIVE IDENTIFICATION REQUIRED FOR AIRPORT CHECK-IN
```

*Example of a Sabre E-ticket Receipt*

# Review

1. What entry code is used to produce tickets from a retrieved PNR?

2. Write the entry to ticket only segments 1, 3, and 5 of an itinerary.

3. Assume a PNR has the following names:

   ```
   1.2FORD/PAUL MR/TINA MRS    2.2CHUNG/RONALD MR/PATRICIA MRS
   ```

   Write the entry to produce a ticket only Patricia Chung.

4. Write the entry to produce a ticket and indicate a check as the form of payment.

5. Write the entry to produce tickets, indicating AZ as the issuing airline.

6. A client will charge a ticket to the credit card AX3003242498761234, expiring October 2018.

7. Write the entry to produce tickets with the text NONREFUNDABLE in the endorsements/ restrictions box.

8. Assume LH is the issuing carrier and the itinerary qualifies for a 9-percent commission rate. Write the entry to ticket the PNR.

# Advance Seat Assignments

## Objectives

*After completing this unit, you should be able to do the following:*

1. Identify the factors that affect passenger seating preference and selection.
2. Request automatic seat assignment by zone and location.
3. Reserve specific seats on a designated segment.
4. Display the seat map for a designated segment or flight.

Sabre can be used by agents to assign prereserved seats on flights operated by specific carriers. On American Airlines flights, seats can be reserved up to 331 days before departure. Passenger seating is referred to by a location code. Depending on the aircraft configuration, the following location codes may be used:

| | |
|---|---|
| A | Aisle |
| W | Window |
| X | Opposite sides of the aisle |
| C | Business class |
| L | Left side of the aircraft |
| R | Right side of the aircraft |
| J | Upper deck (747 aircraft only) |

## Automatic Seat Assignment

The entry code 4G used to request automatic seat assignment on a confirmed flight segment. The zone and location codes are combined to request automatic seat assignment, as follows:

4G<Segment>/<Zone and location>

## Example:
4G2/W

This example requests a prereserved seat on segment 2. The code W is used to request a window seat. If the desired seat type available, Sabre will make the seat assignment automatically. Sabre responds as follows:

```
DONE FLT UA 626Y 10APRAKLLAX  REQUESTED
```

The response indicates the carrier, flight, class, departure date, and city pair. The text on the right indicates that advance seat assignment has been requested from the carrier. In the itinerary, the code HRQ ("have requested seats") is added to the applicable flight segment. (The code HRS is added to American Airlines segments.)

If a PNR has more than one passenger, Sabre will attempt to assign adjacent seats, with one seat in the specified location.

## Smoking Requests

Smoking is not permitted on any domestic flight, or on flights to and from the United States. However, some international carriers, including Air India, Garuda, Philippine Airlines, Royal Jordanian, Pakistan Airlines, and Aeroflot, permit smoking in designated sections of the cabin on some routes. If smoking is permitted, and if prereserved seating is offered, the option codes S and N may be used to request the smoking section and nonsmoking section, respectively. For example, the following entry may be used to request a nonsmoking window seat:

4GA/NW

## Assigning Seats on Multiple Segments

Seat assignments can be requested for multiple segments in the same entry, as follows:

4G1,3,5/A

This example requests an aisle seat on segments 1, 3, and 5.

If the itinerary has fewer than six confirmed segments, the secondary code A may be used to request prereserved seats on all segments, as follows:

4GA/W

This example requests a window seat on all segments for which advance seat assignments are available. However, if the itinerary consists of more than five confirmed segments, a separate segment specification must be input for each segment.

When automatic seat assignment is requested, Sabre attempts to assign the best available seat based on the client's preferences and to distribute the weight of the passengers uniformly over the aircraft. If the requested location or zone is not available, a seat availability map will be displayed.

## Assigning a Specific Seat

A specific seat can be assigned by row and letter, as follows:

4G1/14C

This example will assign seat 14C on the flight in segment 1. Adjacent seats can be assigned in the same entry, as follows:

4G1/14ABC

This example will assign seats 14A, 14B, and 14C on the flight in segment 1. Note that the location or zone are not input when specific seats are assigned.

To determine if a specific seat is available, a seat map can be displayed.

## Seat Maps

A seat map shows the status of all the seats on a particular flight. The seating arrangement depends on the configuration of the aircraft. For example, seats on 727 aircraft are arranged on both sides of a single aisle, whereas on wide-body aircraft such as a Boeing 747 or McDonnell Douglas DC-10, several center seats may be located between two aisles.

The following format may be used to display a seat map on an American Airlines flight:

4G<Segment>*
**Example:**
4G2*

The example above requests a seat availability map for segment 2. The seat map is displayed as follows:

| | | | | | | | | | | | |
|---|---|---|---|---|---|---|---|---|---|---|---|
| | 11 AU | BU | ** | .UH | .U | .U | .U | GUH | ** | .U | .U |
| | 12 . | / | ** | . | / | E | F | / | ** | / | . |
| | 13 . | B | ** | C | D | E | F | . | ** | H | . |
| | 14 / | B | ** | C | D | E | F | G | ** | H | . |
| | 15 . | B | ** | C | D | E | F | / | ** | H | J |
| W | 16 . | B | ** | . | . | . | . | . | ** | H | J | W |
| W | 17 A | B | ** | C | D | E | F | G | ** | H | J | W |
| W | 18 A | B | ** | C | D | E | F | G | ** | H | J | W |
| W | 19 A | B | ** | C | D | E | F | G | ** | H | J | W |
| W | 20 A | B | ** | C | D | E | F | G | ** | H | J | W |
| W | 21 A | B | ** | C | D | E | F | G | ** | H | J | W |

Each row of the seat map is numbered, starting at the front, or forward section, of the cabin. If a seat is available for advance seat assignment, the seat letter is displayed. If a seat has already been reserved, a dot (.) is displayed instead of the seat letter. A slash indicates a seat that has been blocked out for group sales or that are located in the buffer zone between the smoking and no-smoking sections. To assign any of these seats, the agent must obtain permission from the airline. Other codes in the seat map indicate special characteristics, such as a seat that does not recline or a seat that is recommended for handicapped passengers.

The following codes may appear in a seat map display:

| | |
|---|---|
| . | Reserved seat |
| / | Buffer zone or blocked seat |
| U | Undesirable |
| H | Handicapped passengers |
| M | Mobility restricted |
| B | Bulkhead locations |
| X | Emergency exits |
| W | Wing locations |

The following format may be used to display a seat map on a specified flight:

4G*<Carrier><Flight><Class><Date><City pair>

**Example:**
4G*AA241Y5MAYLGALAX

The example above will display the seat map for AA 241 in Y class on 5 May from LGA to LAX.

To display seat maps for other carriers besides American Airlines, the Total Access function must be used to link with the carrier's reservation system. For example, the following entry will display a seat map for SA 831 in Y class on 17 June from MIA to CPT:

¤SA/4G*SA831Y17JUNMIACPT

**Displaying Prereserved Seat Data**

When prereserved seats are requested, the code HRQ is added to the flight segment. When a seat assignment is received from the carrier, the code is changed to HRS, indicating that the passengers hold reserved seats. The seat assignment data may be displayed as follows:

*B

Sabre responds as follows:

```
1 UA 831Y 17JUN DENSFO KK 12C N          1.1 WYATT
```

Note the status KK indicating that the seat assignment has been confirmed by the carrier. In this example, seat 12C has been assigned.

**Canceling Seat Assignments**

If a flight segment is canceled, the corresponding seat assignment is canceled automatically. However, it is also possible to cancel only the seat assignment without affecting the confirmed segment. To cancel an assigned seat, the following format may be used:

4GX<Segment>/<Seat Number>

**Example:**
4GX1/23B

**Off-line Seat Requests**

If an airline does offer advance seat assignment through Sabre, an SSR item may be input to request a seat reservation. For example, the following entry may be used to request an aisle seat in the smoking section:

3SMST/AISLE

The SSR codes NSST (no-smoking section seat) and SMST (smoking section seat) are used in SSR entries. The location should be indicated in the text portion of the entry. There is no guarantee that the carrier will actually provide advance seat assignment.

# Review

1. Write the entry to request an aisle seat in the smoking section for all segments.

2. Write the entry to request a window seat on segment 1.

3. Write the entry to request an aisle seat on all segments.

4. Write the entry to assign seat A in row 23 on segment 3.

5. Write the entry to assign seats D, E, and F in row 14 on segment 2.

6. Write the entry to display the seat map for a flight in segment 2.

7. Write the entry to display a seat map for AA 305 in Y class on 21 March from LHR to JFK.

8. What entry is used to display seat assignment data?

9. Assume seat C in row 14 was previously assigned on segment 3. Write the entry to cancel this seat assignment.

10. Write the entry to assign an aisle seat on segments 2 and 4.

# Queues

## Objectives

*After completing this unit, you should be able to do the following:*

1. Obtain a queue count.
2. Sign in to a queue.
3. Remove, end, or ignore records in a queue.
4. Route records to a designated queue.

A queue is an organized sequence of records that can be accessed in consecutive order. The Sabre queues system is called AAquarius. Each queue has a unique number that identifies its function.

| Number | Queue | Function |
|---|---|---|
| GEN | General messages | General communications. |
| SVR | Supervisory messages | Telex messages, supervisory advice |
| NOT | Notification messages | Notifications from Sabre |
| LMC | Left message to contact | PNRs suspended for a preset interval |
| UTR | Unable to reach | PNRs suspended for a present interval |
| 0 | Basic PNR/urgent | Urgent PNRs (within 24 hours) |
| 1 | Basic PNR/Non-urgent | Non-urgent PNRs |
| 2 | Car/Hotel confirmations | Confirmation numbers for car/hotel segments |
| 5 | Schedule changes | Airline schedule changes within 17 days |
| 6 | Schedule changes | Airline schedule changes beyond 17 days |
| 9 | TAW | Priceable PNRs for ticketing |
| 10 | Ticket suspense | Ticket time limits |
| 11 | Airline rated PNRs | Fares quotes from carriers |
| 12 | Large party | PNRs with 10 or more |
| 14 | Tour desk response | Tour confirmations |
| 17 | Waitlist confirmation | Urgent-within 24 hours |
| 18 | Waitlist confirmation | Beyond 24 hours |
| 19 | Default queue | Unpriceable PNRs |
| 20 | Assigned-special | |
| 21 | Unable to invoice | PNRs with incomplete accounting lines |
| 22 | Corporate travel polic | Modified by AA |
| 23 | Group PNRs | |
| 24 | Boarding pass confirmations | |
| 25 | Boarding pass (unable to confirm) | |
| 26 | Tour time limit | |
| 27 | Rejected BP | |
| 29 | Internet bookings | |

(The function of each queue may be amended from time to time.)

Most queues contain PNRs that require some sort of action. For example, the PNRs in queue 17 require the segment status to be updated, and PNRs in queue 9 have TAW ticketing arrangements for the current date. A record that awaits attention or action in a queue is said to be *on queue*. Accessing the records in a queue is referred to as *working a queue*.

Not all queues contain PNRs. Three queues, called message queues, provide the agency with an electronic mailbox system by which agents can leave text messages on the computer for other agents in the office.

## Queue Counts

A queue count is a summary of the messages or records currently on queue. The entry code QC is used to obtain a queue count, as follows:

QC/<queue number>

**Example:**
QC/17

The example above requests a record count for queue 17, which is used for waitlist clearances. Sabre responds as follows:

```
1044/18MAY B4T0
PNR/Q17    4
```

The first line of the response indicates the time and date of the queue count, and the pseudo-city code of the agency where the count was requested. The second line gives the number of records on queue. In this example, queue 17 has four records on queue.

To obtain a message and record count for all the queues used by the agency, omit the queue number, as follows:

QC/

Sabre responds as follows:

```
GEN....17      5....19
SVR.....2      9....27
UTR.....6      17....2
LMC.....1      23....1
TOTAL MESSAGES........19
TOTAL SPECIAL..........7
TOTAL PNRS............49
```

The response gives the number of messages or records assigned to each queue, along with a summary of the items in the message queues, special queues, and record queues. In the example above, 19 messages are contained in the general and supervisory message queues. The general message queue is indicated by GEN, and the supervisory message queue by SVR.

Seven records are assigned to the special queues, the UTR and LMC queues. The purpose of these queues is discussed later in this chapter. In this queue count, 49 PNRs require special handling in the record queues.

A queue count of the UTR or LMC queue may be obtained as follows:

| | |
|---|---|
| QC/U | Count PNRs in the UTR queue |
| QC/L | Count PNRs in the LTR queue |

Multiple record counts may be requested as follows:

| | |
|---|---|
| QC/1/5 | Count PNRs in queues 1 and 5 |
| QC/1-5 | Count PNRs in queues 1, 2, 3, 4, and 5 |

A slash is typed to separate multiple queue numbers, and a dash is typed to define a range of consecutive queue numbers.

To obtain a queue count from the branch office of a multi-office agency, the office pseudo city code must be included, as follows:

| | |
|---|---|
| QC/B4T0 | All queues at branch office B4T0 |
| QC/B4T0/B4R0 | All queues at branch offices B4T0 and B4R0 |
| QC/B4T017 | Branch office B4T0/queue 17 only |

## Accessing a Queue

To access the records in a queue, the agent must sign in to the queue. The entry code Q is used to sign in to a queue, as follows:

Q/<Queue number>

**Example**:
Q/17

When the agent has signed in to the queue, the first record is displayed automatically. In this example, the first record in queue 17 will be displayed.

To sign into a queue at a branch office, the office pseudo city code must be typed before the queue number, as follows:

Q/B4T09

This example will access the records in queue 9 at branch office B4T0.

**Working a Queue**

When an agent signs into a record queue, the first PNR is displayed automatically. When the transaction is ended, the PNR is removed from the queue, and the next PNR on queue is displayed. If the transaction is ignored, the PNR is moved to the end of the queue.

While the agent is signed in to a queue, no other PNRs can be accessed except the records that are on queue. To perform other duties, the agent must exit from the queue. When the agent exits, the last PNR that was displayed remains in the work area until the transaction is ended or ignored.

While the agent is working a queue, the queue number can be displayed with following entry:

*Q

To remove a PNR from the queue when no action has been taken, the following entry may be used:

QR

When the queue is worked, the following commands may be used to exit the queue:

QXR         Exit queue and removes the last PNR from the work area
QXE         Exit queue and ends the transaction
QXI         Exit queue and ignores the transaction

If the client cannot be contacted to confirm a reservation, the record may be placed on the UTR (Unable to Reach) queue. If a message is left for the client to call back, the PNR may be placed on the LMC (Left Message to Contact) queue. These special queues are used to suspend a PNR for a set time interval. When the interval has expired, the PNR will reappear at the front of the queue from which it was originally suspended.

The time interval for the UTR and LTR queues can be set by the agency. In most cases, the UTR queue is set to suspend a PNR for 15 minutes, and the LTR for 24 hours.

The following entries are used to place a displayed PNR in one of the special queues:

QU         Place PNR in UTR queue
QL         Place PNR in LMC queue

When a PNR is placed in the UTR or LMC queue, the next PNR in the queue is displayed automatically.

## Placing PNRs on Queue

Some records, such as PNRs with waitlist clearances or schedule changes, are placed on queue automatically. The agent can also place a PNR on queue, for special handling. Each agency has several queues that it can use for its own purposes.

When a PNR is placed on queue, a prefatory instruction should be included to advise the agent who works the queue. In the example above, when the agent signed in to queue 3, the prefatory instruction CFM TO PSGR was displayed above the first PNR. Various other messages can also be displayed, depending on the situation. A prefatory instruction code, or PIC, is used to specify the message.

The following format is used to place a PNR on queue:

QP/<Queue number>/<PIC>

**Example:**

QP/34/11

The prefatory instruction code 11 specifies the message SEE REMARKS will be displayed with the PNR, instructing the agent to consult the remarks field for detailed advice or instructions.

The following are examples of common prefatory instruction codes:

| | | |
|---|---|---|
| 1 | CFM TO PSGR | Confirm reservation to passenger |
| 2 | UTR or LMC | Unable to reach, or left message to contact |
| 3 | -UNTKTD PTA- | Unticketed prepaid ticket advice |
| 6 | ASC | Advise client of schedule change |
| 7 | TA | Ticketing arrangement |
| 10 | -CNI PTA- | Contact and issue PTA |
| 11 | SEE REMARKS | Instructions may be found in Remarks Field |
| 12 | CFM FRM LIST | Confirm from waitlist |
| 18 | SPCL MEAL | Special meal request |
| 27 | -FLT CNLD- | Flight cancelled |
| 30 | SKDCHG CKOUT | Schedule change/check out itinerary |
| 33 | FARE CHG | Fare change |
| 41 | UNA TKT | Unable to ticket |
| 59 | RQST FNL PMT | Request final payment |
| 74 | ADV DOCS | Advise documents needed |

Copyright © 2015, Dennis L. Foster

# Review

1. In which queue would an agent find PNRs with urgent waitlist clearance?

2. Which queue contains PNRs with TAW ticketing arrangements for the current date?

3. What entry code is used to obtain a count of records or messages in a queue?

4. What entry code is used to sign into a queue?

5. When an agent signs in to a queue, what is displayed?

6. What entry is used to sign out of a queue and end the transaction?

7. What entry code would be used to obtain a queue count of queue 17 at a branch office with the pseudo city code BW3R?

8. What entry will place the current PNR in the UTC queue?

9. What entry is used to sign out of a queue and ignore the transaction?

10. What entry is used to exit from the queue without ending or ignoring the transaction?

11. Write the entry to display a queue count for all queues.

12. Write the entry to display a queue count for queue 18.

13. Write the entry to access queue 18.

14. Write the entry to place a PNR into queue 35 with prefatory instruction 11.

94

# Client Profiles

## Objectives

*After completing this unit, you should be able to do the following:*

1. Explain the purpose and use of client profiles.
2. Display a primary or secondary STAR.
3. Move mandatory data from a STAR to a PNR.
4. Move selected optional data.
5. Create or update a client profile.

A client profile is a special computer record that contains passenger data items for a frequent traveler. Passenger data can be transferred from a client profile to facilitate the creation of a PNR. SABRE client profiles are called Special Traveler Account Records, or STARs. A STAR may be stored on one of two levels. A level-1 STAR contains data for a primary client, such as a company, government agency, or school district. A level-2 STAR contains data for a passenger associated with a level-1 STAR. For example, a corporation would have a level-1 STAR, but each employee would have a level-2 STAR. A level-1 STAR may have any number of associated level-2 STARS.

## Displaying a STAR

Each STAR has an identification code called the STAR ID code. The ID code of a level-1 STAR may consist of up to 25 alphanumeric characters. The entry code N* is used to display a STAR, as follows:

N*<ID code>

**Example:**
N*ABM

The account name may not contain a slash. The example above will display the level-1 STAR that has the ID code ABM. The STAR is displayed as follows:

```
     ABM
     0S    ABM CORPORATION
     1A    9702-555-1234-A
     2A    9702-555-5432-B
     3A    5/SAMPLE STARS INC
     4A    5/2001 ODYSSEY BLVD
     5A    5/LAS VEGAS NV 89001
     6A    W-DISCOVERY TRAVEL‡1234 BUCKHORN ST‡LAS VEGAS NV 89001
     7O    5-*AX318717171213191‡9/18
     8O    5-CK
     9N    **AUTH TO BK - ALICE OR CHRIS**
```

The header indicates the STAR ID code. Each of the remaining lines has a line number and a one-letter code. Line 0 has the code S, indicating the account name. The other lines have the code A, O, or N. The line code may be one of the following:

| | |
|---|---|
| S | Subject line |
| P | Priority information |
| A | Always used |
| O | Optional data |
| N | Never used |
| R | Restricted |

The line coded S is called the subject line and contains the account name. The code P indicates a priority line that contains important information but is not used in a PNR. The codes A and O indicate lines that contain passenger data items. If a line is coded A, the item is a mandatory item that should always be transferred to the PNR. If a line is coded O, the item is an optional item that may--or may not--be transferred to the PNR, depending on the situation.

If a line is coded N, the data is informational only and is never transferred to the PNR. A line coded R contains restricted data and is also for informational purposes only.

**Determining a STAR ID Code**

To determine a STAR ID code, a list of codes can be displayed, using the first letter or number. The entry code NLIST is used to list STAR ID codes, as follows:

NLIST/<Initial>

**Example:**
NLIST/S

The example above requests all STAR ID codes beginning with the initial S. When an ID list is obtained, a STAR can be displayed from the list, as follows:

N*2

The example above will display the STAR in the second line of the ID list.

**Displaying a Level-2 STAR**

The following format is used to display a level-2 STAR:

N*<Level-1 ID code>–<Level-2 ID code>

**Example:**
N*ABM–SMITH

In the example above, the level-1 STAR has the ID code ABM, and the level-2 STAR has the ID code SMITH. The level-2 ID code may consist of up to 12 characters. This entry will display the profiles for both ABM and SMITH, so that the data items can be transferred to the PNR.

## Moving Data Lines

The following entry will move all the data lines coded A from a displayed STAR to a PNR:

    NM

One or more O lines can also be moved as follows:

    NM8

The example above will copy all the mandatory lines along with optional line 8. The mandatory lines are coded A in the STAR display, and the optional lines are coded O. If an optional line is not specified, only the mandatory lines coded A will be moved to the PNR.

An end-item may be used to move multiple optional lines, as follows:

    NM7Σ9

This example will move optional lines 7 and 9 along with the mandatory lines.

### Excluding Mandatory Lines

The secondary code X can be used to prevent a line that is coded A from transferring to the PNR. For example, the following entry will transfer all mandatory lines except line 2:

    NMX2

An end-item may be used to exclude multiple lines, as follows:

    NMX2ΣX3

This example will transfer all lines that are coded A, except lines 2 and 3. Note that X is typed before each line number to be excluded.

# Review

1. What entry code to is used to display a client profile?

2. What entry would be used to display a list of STARs with the initial B?

3. Write the entry to retrieve a Level-1 STAR named UNISYS.

4. Write the entry to display a Level-2 STAR for passenger Harman associated with a Level-1 STAR named PACTEL.

5. In a displayed profile, what code identifies mandatory data that should always be moved to a PNR?

6. What code identifies optional data that may or may not be moved to a PNR, depending on the situation?

7. What code identifies data that is informational only but is never moved to a PNR?

8. What does the abbreviation STAR signify?

9. Write the entry to move the mandatory data lines from all levels of a displayed STAR.

10. Write the entry to move the mandatory lines from all levels, along with optional lines 7, 9, and 11.

# Hotel Reservations

## Objectives

*After completing this unit, students should be able to do the following:*

1. Display and interpret a hotel index for a specified city.
2. Display a hotel index by rate category, bedding type, or location.
3. Display hotel availability with or without an air itinerary.
4. Display hotel reference points.
5. Display a hotel description.
6. Sell a hotel segment from a description.
7. Input guarantee and deposit information in a hotel segment.
8. Modify an existing hotel segment.
9. Input a direct hotel booking.

The Sabre hotel reservation system is named ShAArp Plus. Each hotel vendor represented in the system is identified by a two-letter code, called the chain code. For example, HI refers to the Holiday Inn chain, and IC refers to the Inter-Continental chain. Independent properties are represented by referral organizations such Best Western (BW) or Utell International (UI).

A complete list of hotel vendors and chain codes may be displayed as follows:

DU*/HTL

The following are examples of major participating hotel vendors:

| | | | |
|----|-------------------|----|------------------------|
| BW | Best Western | DI | Days Inn |
| HH | Hilton (domestic) | HL | Hilton (international) |
| HI | Holiday Inn | HJ | Howard Johnson |
| HY | Hyatt | IC | Inter-Continental |
| MC | Marriott | RA | Ramada |
| SI | Sheraton | TL | Travelodge |
| UI | Utell International | | |

## Room Types and Rates

At most properties, room rates vary based on the room category and bedding. The following codes are commonly used to indicate various room categories:

| | |
|---|-----------------|
| A | Deluxe room |
| B | Superior room |
| C | Standard room |
| D | Discounted rate |
| P | Promotional rate |
| S | Suite |

A bedding code is used with the room category to indicate the number and size of beds. For instance, 1K refers to a room with one king bed, and 2Q refers to a room with two queen beds. The following are examples of common bedding codes:

| | |
|---|---|
| 1K | One king bed |
| 1Q | One queen bed |
| 2Q | Two queen beds |
| 2D | Two double beds |
| 1D | One double bed |
| 2T | Two twin beds |

The codes for the room category and bedding are combined to indicate the room type. For example, A1K refers to a deluxe room with 1 king bed, and B2D refers to a superior room with 2 double beds.

The following are examples of common rate categories:

| | |
|---|---|
| RAC | Rack rates |
| COR | Corporate rates |
| GOV | Government rates |
| MIL | Military rates |
| WKD | Weekend rates |
| SPL | Special rates |
| IND | Industry rate |

Other category codes may also appear, depending on the property or chain. Rack rates are the normal room rates that are offered to the general public. Other categories indicate discounted rates that are offered to special groups or are designed to offset periods of low demand. Some rate categories may require a deposit or guarantee. The following codes are used to indicate guarantee policies:

| | |
|---|---|
| G | Guarantee required |
| D | Deposit required |
| 4 | 4 P.M. hold |
| 6 | 6 P.M. hold |

## Displaying Hotel Availability

The entry code HOT is used to display hotel availability. If an itinerary is present, the following entry may be used:

HOT<Segment>

**Example:**
HOT2

This example requests hotels in the arrival point of segment 2.

*Response:*

```
QUALIFIERS - LHR/12JAN-7NT2/A/C-AUD
+ ACTUAL RATES  E-EXCLUSIVES       DIST  N/C AMENITY   RATE RANGE
  1 SI SHERATON HEATHROW           3SE N    I SFBD      169 - 369
  2 RD RADISSON EDWARDIAN          3SE      I SFBD      189 - 359
  3 RT IBIS HEATHROW               3S  N      S B       100 - 150
  4 MC MARRIOTT WINDSOR            13W       I   BD     129 - 189
  5 RT MERCURE HEATHROW            5S       I S          92 - 185
  6 UI LE CHATEAU                  12W           B R     220 - 220
  7 DI THAMES THISTLE HOTEL        17S           BDR     164 - 184
  8 UI PRINCE EDWARD               9SW           BDR      90 -  90
  9 HI CROWNE PLAZA HEATHROW       5S  N    I SFBD      140 - 220
I-HSPD P-POOL S-FREE SHTL F-FITN B-FREE BKST D-DINE R-FREE PARK
```

Each hotel listing is identified by a line item number and shows the chain code, property code, and property name. The alphanumeric code following the property name is called the mileage/direction indicator and shows the distance and direction of the property from the airport. For example, 3SE indicates that the property is 3 miles southeast of the airport. Amenities and the rate range are also displayed.

The following codes may appear in the amenity list:

| | |
|---|---|
| I | High-speed internet |
| P | Pool |
| S | Free shuttle service |
| F | Fitness centre |
| B | Free breakfast |
| D | Dining |
| R | Free parking |

The display defaults to the currency of the user's country. In this example, rates are displayed in AUD.

## Displaying Hotel Availability by City

If an air itinerary is not in the agent work area, hotel availability can be displayed by city, as follows:

HOT<City>

**Example:**
HOTSFO

The example above requests hotels in San Francisco.
A location may be specified as follows:

HOTSFO/Λ

A slash is typed before the location indicator. This example requests properties near the airport. Other location indicators, such as C (city center) or R (resort area), may also be requested when a hotel index is displayed. For example, the following entry may be used to request hotels in Honolulu, in the resort area:

    HOTHNL/R

A vendor may also be specified, as in the following entry:

    HOTATL/MC

This example requests hotels in Atlanta and specifies the Marriott chain.
    Secondary codes, called qualifiers, may be used to narrow the selection. For example, the qualifier RC is used to specify a rate category, as follows:

    HOTORD/RC-C

In this example, the category code C specifies corporate rates.
    The following rate categories may be requested:

| | | | |
|---|---|---|---|
| C | Corporate | M | Military |
| G | Government | P | Promotional |
| W | Weekend | S | Senior citizen |
| V | Convention | T | Tour/package |
| F | Family plan | | |

Other qualifiers may be used to specify properties with a particular type of room location, a maximum rate, bedding, or a maximum distance from the airport.
    The qualifier L is used to specify properties with a particular room location, as follows:

    HOTMIA/L-OF

This example will display only properties with ocean front rooms.
The following are example of room location qualifiers:

| | |
|---|---|
| /L-OF | Room location - ocean front |
| /L-PS | Room location - poolside |
| /L-SV | Room location - sea view |

The qualifier R is used to request a specify a maximum rate, as follows:

    HOTLAX/R-100

This example will display only properties that have a maximum rate of 100 per night.
    The bedding type may also be specified, as follows:

    HOTGSO/1K

In this example, the bedding code 1K specifies properties that offer rooms with one king bed.

The qualifier D may be used to specify the maximum distance from the airport. For example, the following entry will display hotels in Chicago, requesting properties within 10 miles of the O'Hare airport:

HOTORD/D-10

Multiple qualifiers may be combined in the same entry. For example, assume a client who will travel to Seattle prefers a Hilton property in the city center and requests corporate rates. The following entry will request display only hotels matching this client's requirements:

HOTSEA/HH/C/RC-C

*Examples of Hotel Index Entries*

| | |
|---|---|
| HOTMIA/R-75 | Display hotel index for Miami with specified maximum rate |
| HOTORD/MC/2Q | Display hotel index for Chicago with specified chain and bedding |
| HOTHNL/L-OF/R-150/2Q | Display hotel index for Honolulu with specified room location, maximum rate, and bedding type |

If the stay will exceed one night, the number of nights and number of adults must be specified, as in the following example:

HOT1/3NT2

The entry above will display availability for the date and arrival city of segment 1 for a three-night stay, with two adults per room.

If an air itinerary is not present, the city, arrival date, number of nights, and number of adults must be included, as follows:

HOTDEN/20NOV-3NT2

This entry will display hotel availability in Denver for arrival on 20 November for a three-night stay, with two adults per room.

The check-out date may be input instead of the number of nights, as follows:

HOTLHR/10SEP-17SEP2

The example above requests hotel availability in London, for arrival on 10 September and departure on 17 September, with two adults per room. For a multi-airport city, the code for the arrival airport should be input, to obtain the correct mileage/direction data.

The options that are used with hotel index entries can also be included in a hotel availability entry. For example, assume a client plans to travel to OGG, arriving 2 November and departing 7 November. He prefers the Hilton chain but would like a maximum rate of 100. He desires an ocean front room with two queen beds. Based on this information, the following entry may be used to display hotel availability:

HOTOGG/2NOV-7NOV2/HH/R-100/L-OF/2Q

Multiple qualifiers should be input in the order of the client's preference. For example, if a specified chain is more important than the type of bedding, the chain would be input first.


## Hotel Descriptions

Information about each property is contained in a detailed record called a hotel description. The entry code HOD is used to display descriptions. When date availability is displayed, a description can be displayed for a selected property, as follows:

HOD*<Line>

**Example**:
HOD*1

The example above would display the description for the property in line 1.
    The hotel description is displayed as follows:

```
MC01269 MARRIOTT SALT LAKE CTY              SLC
ADDR-    75 SW TEMPLE RD                     17OCT - 4NT2
         SALT LK CTY UT 84101                SALT LAKE CITY UT
PHONE-   801-531-0800                        ** SELL 0H1|LINENBR
FAX-     801-532-4127              TAXES- 10.822 PCT


1   REGULAR RATE                      170.00 USD   GUAR /C-6P
                                                   SEE - HRD* 1
CONCIERGE RATE * UPGRADED RM -1KNG OR 2DBL- * PRIVATE LOUNGE
 SVC W/COMP CONT.L BKFST IN AM - HOR D.OEUVRES/DESSERT PM*MON-T


2   CORPORATE RATE                    155.00 USD   GUAR /C-6P
                                                   SEE - HRD* 2
CORPORATE RATE * DELUXE ROOM -1 KING OR 2 DOUBLE BEDS-
```

The property name, mailing address, and contact telephone numbers appear at the top of each description. A list of available room types and rates is displayed in the first screen of each hotel description. The following entries may be used to page the display:

|    |         |
|----|---------|
| MD | Move down |
| MU | Move up |

Besides location information and rates, each description also provides information about room options, guest plans, and bed taxes. Room options are indicated by the following codes:

|    |                        |
|----|------------------------|
| RA | Rollaway bed for an adult |
| RC | Rollaway bed for a child |
| CR | Crib |
| EX | Extra adult |

The extra adult charge is incurred if a room is occupied by more than two adults. In some cases, a third guest may be assessed both the rollaway bed charge and the extra adult charge.

Depending on the property, two types of guest plans may be available: a family plan and a meal plan. A family plan permits one to three children to stay in the same room as a parent at no charge. However, the applicable charges may be assessed for any rollaway beds that are required. A meal plan includes one to three daily meals in the room rate.

The following are the most common types of meal plans:

| | |
|---|---|
| American plan | Includes three daily meals |
| Modified American plan | Includes full breakfast and dinner |
| Continental plan | Includes continental breakfast |
| Bermuda plan | Includes full breakfast |
| European plan | Does not include any meals |

A hotel description can also be displayed by property number, as follows:

HOD7724

In this example, the property number is 7724.

**Displaying Chain Policy Information**

Policy information for a specified chain can be obtained as follows:

HODHI

This example will display policy information for the Holiday Inn chain. The chain description is a summary of policies regarding deposits, refunds, extra guests, family plans, credit card acceptance, and for forth.

**Hotel Reference Points**

Often, a client may desire a property located near a particular site or attraction. For instance, a client may wish to stay near an amusement park, a sports arena, or a museum. The entry code HCC may be used to display hotel reference points, as follows:

HCC<State>*<Initial>

**Example:**
HCCUT*M

The example above would display reference points in Utah, with the initial M. Note that the two-letter state code is input to specify the state in which the reference point is located. To illustrate, assume a client will travel to New York and would like to stay at a hotel near Broome Industrial Park. However, the client is unsure of the correct spelling of the reference point. The following entry will display a list of reference points with the initial B:

HCCNY*B

Each reference point has an item number, which can be used to display a hotel index. For example, the following entry would display the hotel inex for Broome Industrial Park:

HOT*3

Note that the display key (*) is typed before the line number.

If the name of the reference point is already known, the following entry may be used to obtain a hotel index without displaying the list:

HOT<State>-<Reference point>

**Example:**
HOTAZ-GRAND CANYON

The example above requests a hotel index for Arizona, near the Grand Canyon. When the index is displayed, the mileage/direction indicator will refer to the specified reference point.

**Foreign Reference Points**

To display reference points in foreign countries, the entry code HCCC is used, as follows:

HCCC/<Country>*<Initial>

**Example:**
HCCC/NO*S

The example above would display reference points in Norway  beginning with the initial "S". One to four letters may be typed after the asterisk.


## Selling Hotel Segments

When a hotel description is displayed, the following format may be used to sell a hotel reservation:

0H1‡<Line number>

**Example:**
0H1‡2

The example above will book one room at the rate in line 2. The digit 1 before the cross (‡) indicates 1 room.

SABRE responds as follows:

```
2 HHL HY SS1 SFO IN12MAR-OUT17MAR  5NT  5523 HYATT REGENCY
3C1K-1/162.00USD/AGT04662245/SI-CF/
```

Hotel segments are labeled HHL and include the chain code, segment status, number of rooms, and hotel city. The booking source is indicated by the agent ARC or IATA number. When the transaction is ended, a message will be transmitted notifying the hotel about the reservation. The hotel will then return a confirmation number to be appended to the hotel segment in the CF field.

**Guarantee Information**

The secondary code /G is used to indicate deposit or guarantee information, as follows:

0H1‡3/GDPST

This example indicates that a deposit will be sent to the hotel to guarantee the reservation. If a credit card is used to guarantee a reservation, the information is input as follows:

0H1‡3/GAX3002543100219989EXP 10 18-POWELL

Note that EXP is typed before the expiration date. In the date, only the digits for the day and the last two digits of the year are typed, separated by a space. A space is also typed before the day. The credit card in this example is an American Express card, expiring October 2018. The cardholder's surname, preceded by a slash, is input after the expiration date.

The following codes are used for other means of guaranteeing a hotel reservation:

| GT | Travel agency address |
|---|---|
| GC | Company address |
| GH | Client home address |
| GCR | Corporate number |
| GAGT | Travel agency ARC/IATA number |

**Room Options**

When a hotel segment is sold, a room option such as a rollaway bed or crib can be requested, as follows:

0H1‡3/EX-1

A dash (-) is typed after the option and before the number. The example above indicates that one extra guest will occupy the room. An adult rollaway is requested as follows:

0H1‡3/EX-1/RA-1

# Modifying Hotel Segments

The entry code HOM is used to modify an existing hotel reservation, as follows:

HOM<Segment><Field>/<New Data>

**Example:**
HOM2R/1A1KRAC-1

In the example above, the code R indicates the room information field. This entry would modify a hotel reservation in segment 2 to change the room type to A1KRAC, with one adult. The number of adults is mandatory, even if the number is unchanged.

The code O is used to add or modify the room option field, as follows:

HOM2O/EX-1/RA-1

This entry indicates one extra guest and requests one adult rollaway bed. The existing reservation is segment 2.

The code D is used to modify the date field, as follows:

HOM5D/10MAY-15MAY

This entry would change the arrival and departure dates of a hotel reservation in segment 5.

## Direct Bookings

If a hotel reservation is not booked through SABRE, the hotel segment can still be entered in the itinerary for reference. For instance, an agent might telephone a hotel reservation center to book a reservation at a particular property. In this case, the following format must be used to enter the direct booking in the itinerary:

0HHTAAHK<Rooms><City><In-out>/<Prop.>/<Type>/<Rate>/<Guar. info.> /SI<Adress and phone>/CF-<Conf. number>

**Example:**
0HHTAAHK1BOSIN20APR-OUT21APR/COLONNADE HOTEL/DBLB/65.00/G-DPST /SI-120 HUNTINGTON AVE#NOSTON MA 021116#FONE 617-424-7000 /CF-1295TG

In this example, the property address and phone are input with the secondary code /SI, and the verbal confirmation number is input with /CF. The supplementary information (SI) and confirmation (CF) fields are optional.

The following room type codes are commonly used in direct hotel segments:

| | |
|---|---|
| SGLB | Single room with bath |
| DBLB | Double room with bath |
| QUAD | Quadruple room |
| TRPB | Triple room with bath |
| TWNB | Twin with bath |

One of the following rate categories may be input instead of the rate:

| | |
|---|---|
| MAXR | Maximum rate |
| MODR | Moderate rate |
| MINR | Minimum rate |

# Review

1. Write the entry to display the hotel index for Nice (NCE).

2. Write the entry to display Hilton International properties in Nairobi (NBO).

3. Write the entry to display hotels near the Madrid (MAD) airport.

4. Write the entry to display hotel availability after segment 1, for a 3-night stay for one adult.

5. Write the entry to display hotel availability in Frankfurt (FRA) for 2 adults arriving on 12 June and departing on 17 June.

6. Assume you have obtained the following partial hotel availability display:

```
QUALIFIERS - SLC/17JUN-4NT2/C-USD
+ ACTUAL RATES  E-EXCLUSIVES      DIST  N/C AMENITY  RATE RANGE
  1 HI SALT LAKE CITY DWTN         8SE     IP   D      79 - 149
  2 MC MARRIOTT SALT LAKE CTY      7E      IP F D     155 - 205
  3 QI QUALITY CITY CENTER         7W      I    DR     59 -  85
  4 IP THE BLACKSMITH INN        240N           R      75 -  75
  5 BE HOMESTEAD SUGARHOUSE       10SE          R      44 -  69
  6 FX MOTEL 6 WEST                5N           R      45 -  45
```

What entry will display a hotel description for the Quality City Center?

7. Assume a hotel description is displayed and you want to book a room at the rate in line 2. The client will guarantee the reservation with an American Express card. The account number is 334659870917863, expiring July 2015. The cardholder's surname is Davis. Write the correct entry to sell the hotel segment.

8. What entry will book a room at the rate in line 3 of a hotel description?

9. Assume you want to book a room at the rate in line 5. A child roll-away is requested. Write the correct entry to sell the hotel segment.

10. Write the entry to modify a hotel reservation in segment 2 to change the room type to a deluxe room with 2 queen beds for 2 adults.

11. Write the entry to modify segment 3 to change the request an infant cot (crib).

12. What entry will display policy information for the Inter-Continental chain?

13. Write the entry to display hotel reference points in Spain (ES) beginning with the letter P.

109

# Car Rentals

## Objectives

*After completing this unit, you should be able to do the following:*

1. Identify common car type codes.
2. Display car availability by segment.
3. Display car availability by pickup date, city, and segment.
4. Book a car rental from a car availability display.
5. Obtain a car rental rate quotation.
6. Display an index of car rental outlets in a designated city.
7. Alter the rate display to change the car type, date, location, or vendor.
8. Display competitive prices in a rate shopper display.
9. Book a car rental from a rate quotation.
10. Enter optional data in a car rental booking.
11. Modify a car segment.

Any type of rental vehicle that can be booked through a CRS may be referred to as a car. The Sabre car rental system is named Cars Plus. Car vendors that participate in the Cars Plus system are identified by two-letter codes. The following are examples of major car rental vendors that permit reservations to be booked through Sabre:

| | | | |
|---|---|---|---|
| AI | American International | AJ | Ajax |
| AL | Alamo | ED | Eurodollar |
| ZE | Hertz | ZI | Avis |
| ZL | National | ZN | General |
| ZR | Dollar | ZT | Thrifty |
| ZS | Sears | ZD | Budget |

## Car Type Codes

Car type codes are based on the following elements:

| Size | Type | Shift | Air Conditioning |
|---|---|---|---|
| E  economy | B  car/2 door | A  automatic    R  yes | |
| C  compact | C  car/2 or 4 door | M  manual    N  no | |
| I  intermediate | D  car/4 door | | |
| S  standard | L  limousine | | |
| F  full size | V  van | | |
| L  luxury | T  convertible | | |
| M  mini | S  sports car | | |
| P  premium | F  4-wheel drive | | |
| X  special | X  special | | |
| | W  wagon | | |

111

These elements may be combined to indicate a particular car type. For instance, ECAR signifies an economy car with two or four doors, automatic shift, and air conditioning.

The following are examples of common car types:

| | |
|---|---|
| ECAR | Economy car/automatic shift/air conditioning |
| ECMR | Economy car/manual shift/air conditioning |
| CCAR | Compact car/automatic shift/air conditioning |
| ICAR | Intermediate car/automatic shift/air conditioning |
| SCAR | Standard car/automatic shift/air conditioning |
| SWAR | Standard wagon/automatic shift/air conditioning |
| LCAR | Luxury car/automatic shift/air conditioning |
| XXAR | Special request/automatic shift/air conditioning |

The car types ECAR, CCAR, ICAR, and SCAR may be abbreviated; e.g. EC.

## Car Rate Displays

The basic car availability display shows the vendors and car types that are available, but not the rental rates. Two entry codes may be used to display availability with rates:

| | |
|---|---|
| CQ | Car rate quote |
| CF | Car fare shopper |

The entry code CQ is used to request the rates offered by a specified vendor. To obtain a rate quote, the pickup date, return date, pickup time, and return time are required. If an air itinerary is present, the following format may be used to obtain a rate quote:

CQ<Arrival segment>/<Departure segment<Vendor>

**Example:**
CQ2/3ZD

The example above will display rates offered by Budget (ZD) for the arrival point of segment 2. The pickup date and time will be obtained from segment 2, and the return date and time will be obtained from segment 3.

To display a rate quote without an air itinerary, the following format may be used:

CQ<Vendor><City>/<Pickup date>-<Return date>/<Pickup time>-<Return time>

**Example:**
CQZILHR/10MAY-15MAY/2P-10A

The example above will display rates for Avis . The vehicle will be picked up at London-Heathrow on 10 May at 2P and returned on 15 May at 10A Note that a slash is typed before the pick-up date and after the return date.

A car type may be specified as follows:

CQZILHR/10MAY-15MAY/2P-10A/CC

This entry requests car rates for compact cars (CC).
  A rate plan may be specified, as follows:

CQZILHR/10MAY-15MAY/2P-10A/EC/W

In this example, the code W specifies weekly rates. The following rate plans may be requested:

D        Daily rates
W        Weekly rates
M        Monthly rates
E        Weekend rates

A rate category may also be specified, as follows:

CQZILHR/10MAY-15MAY/2P-10A/EC/P

In this entry, promotional rates are requested. If a rate category is not specified, standard rates will be displayed. The following rate categories may be requested:

S or STD        Standard
P or PRO        Promotional
A or ASC        Association
G or GOV        Government
I or IND        Industry
C or COR        Corporate
U or CNU        Consortium
B or BUS        Business
C or CNV        Convention
P or PKG        Package
C or CRE        Credential

The following is an example of a car rate quote display:

```
ZI AVIS              RATES RETURNED VIA DIRECT CONNECT
DENVER               IN TERMINAL
                     16JUN WED     5P    CORPORATE LOCATION
                     18JUN FRI     2P    RENTAL  2 DAYS   0HRS
-------------------------------------------------------------
          R C USD RATE/PLAN  MI           CHG      APPROX
  1 ECAR          40.99D     UNL          .00       92.12
  2 ECAR          42.99D     UNL          .00       96.52
  3 ECAR          44.99D     UNL          .00      102.14
  4 CCAR          49.99D     UNL          .00      112.48
  5 ICAR          54.99D     UNL          .00      119.45
  6 SCAR          57.99D     UNL          .00      127.50
```

Each line of the display is numbered and shows the car type, rate, and plan. The mileage allowance appears in the MI column, and the excess mileage charge is displayed in the CHG column. The cars in this display offer unlimited mileage, and, thus, no mileage charge is indicated. The approximate total cost is displayed on the right.

A pick-up location other than an airport outlet is called an off-terminal location. The entry code CQL is used to list off-terminal locations, as follows:

CQLZEATL

The example above would list Hertz locations in Atlanta. An area may be specified as follows:

CQLZEATL/C

In this example, the indicator C requests locations in the city center area. Other area indicators include R (resort) and S (suburban).

When a vendor location list is displayed, a rate quote may be obtained as follows:

CQ*<Line>/<Pickup date>-<Return date>/<Pickup time-<Return time>

**Example:**
CQ*3/10SEP-14SEP/2P-11A

The example above requests a rate quote for the location in line 3. In the example above, the rates for pickup at the Marriott Marquis hotel would be displayed.

**Rate Shopper Displays**

A rate shopper display gives the lowest available rates offered by all participating vendors in a specified market. The rates are listed from least expensive to most expensive. As with a vendor rate quote, the pickup date, pickup time, return date, and return time are required to obtain the display. If an air itinerary is present, a rate shopper display can be obtained from a flight segment, as follows:

CF1/2

This example will display low-to-high rates for the arrival point of segment 1, obtaining the pickup date and time from segment 1 and the return date and time from segment 2.

A car type may be specified as follows:

CF1/2/CC

In this example, the car type CC is used to request the rates for compact cars. The following is an example of a rate shopper display:

```
ATLANTA                21AUG WED    3P
                       27AUG TUE   10A  RENTAL  6DAYS  0HRS
-----------------------------------------------------------
                       R C USD RATE/PLAN MI/KM   CHG   APPROX
 1 AL ALAMO     CCMR 00      102.99W    UNL     .00   118.44
 2 AL ALAMO     CCAR 00      109.99W    UNL     .00   121.50
 3 ZI AVIS      CCMR 10      121.95W    UNL     .00   134.56
 4 ZI AVIS      CCAR 10      132.95W    UNL     .00   145.18
 5 ZD BUDGET    CCMR 10      137.97W    UNL     .00   149.48
 6 ZL NATIONAL  CCAR 05      137.99W    UNL     .00   149.50
 7 ZD BUDGET    CCAR 10      158.97W    UNL     .00   172.24
 8 ZL NATIONAL  CCAR 05      158.99W    UNL     .00   172.35
```

Each line shows the vendor code and name, car type code, commission, rate, plan, mileage allowance, excess mileage charge, and approximate total cost. In this example, the lowest weekly rate is offered by Alamo for a compact car with 2 or 4 doors, manual shift, and air conditioning.

If an air itinerary is not present, or if the pickup date and time differ from the arrival information in the itinerary, the pick-up point must be specified along with the rental dates and times, as follows:

CFFRA/12JUL-16JUL/10A-9A/SC

The following secondary codes may be used to obtain a rate shopper display:

UN      Unlimited mileage
FM      Free miles
TM      Time and mileage

For example, the following entry will request only rates that include unlimited mileage:

CFFRA/12JUL-16JUL/10A-9A/SC/UN

A vendor rate quote can be displayed from a rate shopper display, as follows:

CF*3

This example will display a rate quote for the vendor in line 3 of the rate shopper display.

## Displaying Car Rules

When a rate shopper display has been obtained, the rules governing each rate can be displayed as follows:

CF*R1

The example above will display the rules for the rate in line 1 of the rate shopper display. The rules display appears as follows:

```
DATE OF PICKUP       - 22MAR     - TUESDAY
DATE OF RETURN       - 27MAR     - SUNDAY
RATE                 - USD  39.99  100F   .10   DAILY
XTRA DAY/HOUR        - USD XD      XH 7.99  10F
ADVANCE BOOKING      - 1DAY
MINIMUM DAYS         - 1
MAXIMUM DAYS         - 14
PICKUP AFTER         - 0600
RETURN BY            - 2400
OVERNIGHT REQUIRED   - MONDAY
RATE CODE            -SUPDAY
```

## Selling Car Segments

When car rental rates are displayed, the following format may be used to sell a car segment:

0C<line>

**Example:**
0C1

The example above will book a car rental at the rate in line 1 of the rate display. This entry can be used to sell a reservation from either a rate quote or a rate shopper display.

The following is an example of a car segment:

```
3 CAR ZI 21MAR J SS1 ATL/24MAR/ICAR/BS-4665545/CF-
```

The car segment shows the vendor, pick-up date, and week day. The segment status SS1 indicates that a reservation will be confirmed for one vehicle. The pickup point, return date, and car type are also shown. The booking source (BS) is identified by the agency's IATA number. When the transaction is ended, a message will be transmitted to notify the vendor about the booking. The vendor will send back a confirmation number, which will be appended to the car segment in the CF field.

To book more than one car, the number of cars is included as follows:

0C1.2

This example will book 2 cars from line 1 of a rate display.

**Optional Data**

Optional data may be included in a car sell entry, as follows:

0C1/ID-1233456

In this example, the secondary code ID is used to input an identification number, such as a Hertz #1 Club account or a frequent traveler number.

The following are other secondary codes that may be used to input optional data:

| | |
|---|---|
| ARR- | Arrival information |
| W- | Written confirmation |
| CD- | Corporate discount number |
| RT- | Rate input by agent (not guaranteed) |
| IR- | Itinerary remarks |
| PH- | Outlet phone number |
| SI- | Service information |

## Modifying Car Segments

The entry code CM is used to modify an existing car segment as follows:

CM3/CF-77049872001

This example will add a confirmation number to a car reservation in segment 3. The field identifier CF is used to input the confirmation number. This procedure might be required if a car segment was not booked through SABRE and a verbal confirmation number was received by telephone.

Other field identifiers that may be used to modify car segments include the following:

| | | | |
|---|---|---|---|
| PD | Pickup date | CT | Car type |
| RD | Return date | CD | Corporate discount number |
| DO | Return city | SI | Service information |
| PUP | Pickup location | ARR | Arrival time |
| PH | Phone number | ID | Customer I.D. number |
| DOC | Return charge | BS | Booking source |

**Examples of Car Modification Entries**

| | |
|---|---|
| CM2/PD-18JUL | Change pickup date of segment 2 |
| CM3/BS-98076543 | Add booking source to segment 3 |
| CM2/PD-23MAR/CT-ECAR | Change pickup date and car type |

## Displaying Vendor Policies

The entry code CP* is used to display vendor policies, as follows:

CP*ZESFO

The example above will display policies for Hertz in San Francisco. The system responds as follows:

```
HERTZ    --    SAN FRANCISCO AIRPORT   -- IN-TERMINAL
ADDRS-SAN FRANCISCO INTERNATIONAL AIRPORT
      19982 AIRPORT BLVD
      BURLINGAME, CA 94128
PHONE-*415-555-1001-AIRPORT OPERATIONS/NO
      RESERVATIONS
      415-555-4321-UA TERMINAL COUNTER
      415-555-3003-INTERNATIONAL TERMINAL
HOURS-EVERY DAY FROM 0630AM TO 1200MIDNITE
INSUR-OPTIONAL ON ALL TYPES EXCEPT LCAR/PSAR
PAI  -PERSONAL ACCIDENT INSURANCE 7.95/DAY
CDW  -COLLISION DAMAGE WAIVER 7/95/DAY
GAS  -TANKS SHOULD BE RETURNED FULL. OTHERWISE, A
      LOCALLY DETERMINED CHARGE WILL BE ADDED TO
      THE FINAL BILL.
```

The following codes may be used to display only a specified category:

| | |
|---|---|
| PH | Phone |
| H | Hours |
| I | Insurance |
| PA | Personal Accident Insurance |
| CD | Collision Damage Waiver |
| TA | Taxes |
| G | Gasoline allowance/charges |
| EX | Express return |
| S | Shuttle (airport transportation) |
| PY | Payment policies |
| V | Valid credit cards |
| CO | Commissions |
| EQ | Equipment |
| O | Other |
| D | Return points allowed |
| M | Makes of vehicles |
| R | Rules |
| F | Facts |

For example, the following entry will display only the vendor phone number and hours of operation for Avis in San Francisco:

CP*ZISFO/PH/H

# Review

1. Write the entry to display a car quote for Hertz, using the arrival information in segment 5 and the departure information in segment 6.

2. Write the entry to display a rate shopper display using the arrival information in segment 2 and the departure information in segment 3.

3. Assume a client will pick up a car in Miami at 9A on 21 August and return it at 10A on 25 August. He prefers an economy car with 2 or 4 doors. Write the entry to display a rate shopper display.

4. Assume you want to display a car quote for Avis using the date information in segments 1 and 2. The client prefers an intermediate car. Write the correct entry.

5. Write the entry to display car rules for the rate in line 2 of a rate shopper display.

6. Write the entry to display a policy description for Budget at London Gatwick Airport.

7. Write the entry to sell a car from line 3 of a rate display.

8. Write the entry to sell 1 car from line 6, and include the customer number 702635.

9. Write the entry to modify a car rental in segment 5 to change the car type to an economy car with 2 or 4 doors, manual shift, and air conditioning.

10. Write the entry to modify a car rental in segment 3 to change the pick-up date to 17 June.

# Miscellaneous Entries

## Objectives

*After completing this unit, you should be able to do the following:*

1. Verify flight information.
2. Use the calculator and calendar functions.
3. Display weather reports and forecasts.
4. Display currency exchange data and convert currencies.

## Flight Verification

The flight information function, called flifo, is used to verify the routing, departure and arrival times, meal service, equipment, and total flight time of a specified flight. The entry code V* is used for flight verification, as follows:

V*<Carrier><Flight>/<Date>

**Example:**
V*DL1904/12MAR

The example above will display flight information for DL 1904 operating on 12 March. The entry code 2 may also be used for flight verification, as in the following example:

2AA712/24JUN

Sabre responds as follows:

```
210CT       DPTR     ARVL     MEALS S EQP   ELPD   ACCUM  MILES
SEA SFO     805A     955A     B       DC8   1.50   1.50   872
SFO MIA     1100A    847P     L             8.37   9.42   3024
```

The flight in this example originates in SEA, flies two segments, and terminates in MIA. The headings in the flifo display indicate the following information:

| | |
|---|---|
| DPTR | Departure time |
| ARVL | Arrival time |
| MEALS S | Meals served |
| EQP | Aircraft equipment |
| ELPD | Elapsed flight time |
| ACCUM | Accumulated travel time |
| MILES | Total miles flown |

The elapsed flight time shows the total time that the aircraft is in flight. The accumulated travel time shows the total time from the originating point to the terminating point, including time spent on the ground.

If an air itinerary is present, flight information can be verified by segment reference, as follows:

> VI*2

This example will display flight information for segment 2. Multiple segments may be specified as follows:

> VI*2/4/6

Flight information can also be obtained from an availability display as follows:

> VA*1

This example will display flight information for line 1 of an availability display.

## Participating Vendors

A participating vendor is any travel company, such as an airline, hotel, car rental company, or ship line, that permits bookings to be made through Sabre. The entry code DU*/ is used to display a list of participating vendors by category, as follows:

DU*/<Category>

**Example:**
DU*/HTL

A three-letter keyword is used to specify the category. In the example above, the keyword HTL indicates hotel vendors. The following are examples of commonly used keywords for participating vendors.

| | |
|---|---|
| CAR | Car rental companies |
| HTL | Hotels |
| BUS | Buslines |
| RAL | Railways |
| SEA | Shiplines |

A list of participating vendors is called a vendor table.

To illustrate, assume an agent desires to display a list of railway vendors that permit reservations to be booked through Sabre. Using the keyword RAL, the following entry may be used to display the vendor table:

DU*/RAL

# Minimum Connecting Times

When a passenger must change aircraft in a connecting city, the minimum connecting time may vary depending on the airport. The minimum connecting time must be sufficient to allow the passenger to disembark, proceed to the boarding gate, and board the connecting flight.

The entry code T*CT- is used to display the minimum connecting times at a specified airport, as follows:

    T*CT-GEG

The example above will display minimum connecting times at the Spokane, Washington airport (GEG). The following is an example of a connecting time display:

```
STANDARD   D/D...D/I...I/D...I/I
ONLINE      .30   1.00  1.00  1.00
OFFLINE     .40   1.00  1.00  1.00
CO-CZ DD    .40
UA-UA DD    .20
DL-DL DD    .20
NW-NW DD    .25
CO-CO DD    .15
```

The first line indicates the type of connection. The following codes are used in the header:

| | |
|---|---|
| D/D | Domestic-to-domestic |
| D/I | Domestic-to-international |
| I/D | International-to-domestic |
| I/I | International-to-international |

The two lines below the header give the minimum connecting times for on-line and off-line connections. An on-line connection is a change of flights operated by the same airline. An off-line connection requires the passenger to change to a different airline. If the flight gates in an off-line connection are located in different airport terminals, the minimum connecting time is usually greater.

Connecting times may also be displayed for specific carriers, as illustrated in the example above. The time is given in hours and minutes. In the example, the minimum connecting time is 30 minutes for on-line domestic-to-domestic connections and one hour for on-line domestic-to-international connections. For on-line connections operated by Delta, the minimum connecting time is 20 minutes.

The connecting time for specific carriers may be requested as follows:

    T*CT-GEG/COCZ

This example will display the minimum connecting time at GEG for connections from CO to CZ.

## Weather Information

Weather information may be obtained by means of the entry code ¤WEA. To obtain U.S. National Weather Service information for a particular city, the secondary code WX* is input, as follows:

¤WEA/WX*<City>

**Example:**
¤WEA/WX*PHX

Either a city code or an airport code may be used in this entry. The following is an example of a weather information display:

```
NATIONAL WEATHER SERVICE - APR 21
CURRENT                 FORECAST        FORECAST
 2:20 P MT              TUE.....APR 22  WED.....APR 23
WEA      TEMP    WIND   WEA   HI/LO      WEA   HI/LO
CLEAR    89      W  8   SUNNY 92/74    SUNNY 95/76
```

The weather information is based on the last reported temperature and weather conditions and covers a two-day period.

To obtain a descriptive city forecast, the secondary code CF is input, as in the following example:

¤WEA/CF*PHX

Each city forecast covers a three-day period.

The secondary code EF may be used to obtain an extended regional forecast, as follows:

¤WEA/EF*NYC

The extended forecast covers a five-day period.

If a forecast is requested for an international city, weather information will be displayed for the entire geographic area. Either the city code or the airport code may be used to obtain a forecast.


## Calculator Functions

The calculator function is used to perform an arithmetic operation, such as adding, subtracting, multiplying, or dividing. A symbol or sign that is used to perform arithmetic is called an operator. The following arithmetic operators are used with the calculator function:

| | |
|---|---|
| ‡ | Add |
| — | Subtract |
| * | Multiply |
| / | Divide |

The entry code T¤ is used for arithmetic operations. As an example, the following entry will add 225 and 18:

T¤225‡18

Besides arithmetic, the calculator function can also be used add or subtract days from a calendar date, as follows:

T¤12NOV–21

This entry will subtract 21 days from November 12.

The same entry code can also be used to display a calendar for a specified month. For instance, to display a calendar for June, 1999, the following entry would be used:

T¤JUN/99

Dates can be displayed for a specified day of the week, as well. As an example, the following entry may be used to determine the date of each Friday in December, 2007:

T¤FR/DEC07

In this entry, the day of the week must be indicated by the two letters.

The secondary code ET may be used to calculate elapsed time. The arrival point and departure point must be specified for each time, as follows:

T¤ET845PSFO–610AANC

This entry requests the elapsed time from 845P San Francisco time to 610A Anchorage time.

**Quick Fare Calculation**

The entry code W/ may be used to determine the base fare and tax from a total fare, as follows:

W/359

Note that the dollar sign or currency code must not be typed in this entry.
Sabre responds as follows:

        326.36/32.64

In this example, the base fare is $326.36, and the U.S. transportation tax is $32.64. Cents will be included in the response, even if they are omitted in the fare calculation entry.

The secondary code B may be used to calculate the tax and total fare from a base fare, as follows:

W/B298.18

The code B is typed before the amount to indicate that the amount is a base fare. When this entry is input, Sabre will respond as follows:

        **29.82/328.00**

In this example, the tax is 29.82, and the total fare is 328.00.

**Time Checks**

The entry code T* can be used to determine the local time in a specified city, as follows:

T*<City or airport code>

**Example:**
T*LHR

The example above requests the local time in London. Note in this example that the airport code LHR is input for the London-Heathrow airport.

# Currency Rates

The entry code DC is used to display currency exchange rates based on the bank buying rate. The data is updated weekly to reflect changes in the international exchange rate. The following entry is used to display currency conversion rates:

DC*<Currency>

**Example:**
DC*AUD

Either the three-letter currency code or the country name may be input to display the exchange rate. When this entry is input, Sabre responds as follows:

| COUNTRY | CURRENCY | CODE | DEC. | RATE | EFF DATE | NEW RATE |
|---------|----------|------|------|------|----------|----------|
| AUSTRALIA | DOLLAR | AUD | 2 | 1.8569 | 10AUG | 1.8571 |

The response gives the country, currency name, and ISO currency code. The dec column indicates the number of decimals that are used in the currency. A number from 1 to 3 may appear in this column.

**ISO Currency Codes**

The following are examples of ISO currency codes:

| Country | Currency | Code |
|---|---|---|
| Argentina | Peso | ARS |
| Australia | Dollar | AUD |
| Austria | Euro | EUR |
| Belgium | Euro | EUR |
| Canada | Dollar | CAD |
| Denmark | Krone | DKK |
| France | Euro | EUR |
| Germany | Euro | EUR |
| Hong Kong | Dollar | HKD |
| India | Rupee | INR |
| Ireland | Euro | EUR |
| Italy | Euro | EUR |
| Japan | Yen | JPY |
| Luxembourg | Euro | EUR |
| Netherlands | Euro | EUR |
| New Zealand | Dollar | NZD |
| Portugal | Euro | EUR |
| South Africa | Rand | ZAR |
| Spain | Euro | EUR |
| Sweden | Krona | SEK |
| Switzerland | Franc | CHF |
| Taiwan | Dollar | TWD |
| United Kingdom | Pound | GBP |
| United States | Dollar | USD |

Exchange rates can be displayed by country name, as follows:

DC*AUSTRALIA

To display the exchange rates for all international currencies, the code CUR is input instead of a currency code, as follows:

DC*CUR

The entry code DC displays the current bank buying rate. To display the current market rate, the entry code DZ may be used as follows:

DZ*FRANCE

## Currency Conversion

To convert an amount from one currency to another, the following format may be used:

DC‡<Currency><Amount>/<Currency>

**Example:**
DC‡GBP245.50/CAD

The example above will convert 245.50 British pounds to Canadian dollars.

If the currency code of the amount to be converted is omitted, Sabre will apply the currency of the country where the terminal is located.

# Review

1. What entry would be used to display flight information for BA 42 departing on 12 May?

2. What entry will display flight information for the flight in line 4 of an availability display?

3. Write the entry to display flight information for segment 3 of an itinerary.

4. What entry will display minimum connecting times at Charles de Gaulle airport?

5. Write the entry to display the date 28 days before 12 May.

6. What entry will display the exchange rate for Japanese yen?

7. Write the entry to convert NZD 1750 to CAD.

8. What entry will display the local time in JNB?

# Phase IV Ticketing

## Objectives

*After completing this unit, you should be able to do the following:*

1. Create a manual ticket record.
2. Enter price and ticketing information in a ticket record.
3. Store a ticket record.
4. Issue tickets from a manual ticket record.

Although SABRE can correctly autoprice most domestic and many international itineraries, occasionally, the fare information must be entered by the agent. This situation may occur if a carrier's fares or routes are not stored in the SABRE database, or if the routing is too complex to autoprice. In these cases, the agent must manually enter all the information required to fare the itinerary. This procedure is referred to as Phase IV pricing and ticketing. PNRs with itineraries priced by the manual method must be ticketed using a special format.

The Phase IV function is used to create a ticket record for PNRs with itineraries that SABRE cannot price. The fare information may then be inserted into the ticket record manually. In general, the following information may be inserted:

1. Line entitlement (fare basis)
2. Fare calculation
3. Agency commission
4. Base fare and tax

Depending on the itinerary, other fare information may also be inserted, such as a tour code, validity dates, endorsement/restrictions, and international fare information.

## Creating a Ticket Record

The following format is used to create a ticket record:

W‡C

To illustrate, assume SABRE cannot price the following itinerary:

```
1 DL1236Y 12JUN 1 ATLMCI HK1  927A 1030A
2 UA 247Q 19JUN 1 MCIORD HK1  725A  849A
3 WN 234Q 19JUN 1 ORDPHX HK1 1245P  152P
```

The following entry may be used to create a ticket record:

W‡C

SABRE responds as follows:

```
     FAIL CODE - 02
     TA-ADT
     1 O ATL DL1236Y  12JUN   927A OK
     2 O MCI UA 247Q  19JUN   725A OK
     3 O ORD WN 234Q  19JUN  1245P OK
        PHX
```

Pricing qualifiers may be added to the entry to specify the passenger type, or segment selection. For example, to create separate ticket records for adult and child passengers, the passenger types may be included, as in the following example:

W‡C‡PADT/CHD

To ticket only a portion of the itinerary, segment selection may be included, as in the following entry:

W‡C‡S1/3/4

Name selection may also be included as follows:

W‡C‡N1.2

Pricing qualifiers may be combined in one entry as follows:

W‡C‡N2.1‡S1/3

## Inserting Data in the Ticket Record

When a ticket record has been created, the next step is to insert the required fare information. At a minimum, the record must include the fare basis, base fare and tax, agency commission, and fare calculation.

The following secondary action codes identify the fare information to be inserted in a ticket record:

| | |
|---|---|
| L | Line entitlement |
| C | Fare calculation |
| K | Commission |
| Y | Base fare/tax |
| U | Tour code |
| * | Validity dates |
| RF | Routing - foreign |
| RD | Routing - domestic |
| RT | Routing - transborder |

The entry code W‡I is used to insert information in the ticket record. A secondary action code is input to designate the type of information that is to be inserted.

## Inserting the Fare Basis

The secondary action code L is used to insert the fare basis for each segment as follows:

W‡I‡L<Line>-<Fare Basis>

**Example:**
W‡I‡L1-Y

The example above inserts the fare basis Y for segment 1. Multiple segments with the same fare basis may be indicated as follows:

   W‡I‡L2/3-Q

This entry inserts the fare basis Q for segments 2 and 3.

To insert different fare bases for multiple segment lines, separate each fare basis with a cross as follows:

   W‡I‡L1-Y‡L2/3-Q

The fare basis codes will be printed on the ticket in the fare basis box on each line of the itinerary. These codes are referred to as the line entitlement.

## Inserting Validity Dates

Validity dates are printed in the NOT VALID BEFORE/AFTER box on the passenger ticket. The dates are inserted in the ticket record along with the line entitlement.

   W‡I‡L<Fare basis>*<Validity Dates>

**Example:**
W‡I‡L1-YXIT21*10MAY01JUN

In the example above, the fare basis YXIT21 in segment 1 is valid from 10 May through 1 June.

## Inserting a Commission

An agency commission, if applicable, may also be inserted in the ticket record. The secondary action code KP is used to insert the commission as a percentage.

   W‡I‡KP<Pct>

**Example:**
W‡I‡KP2

If the commission is entered as a dollar amount, the K should be used instead, as in the following example:

W‡I‡K24.00

The percentage or amount will be printed in the commission box on the ticket. If a commission is not entered in the ticket record, it will not be printed on the ticket.

**Inserting the Fare Calculation**

The fare calculation is inserted with the secondary code C as follows:

W‡I‡C<Fare Calculation>

**Example:**
W‡I‡CJKT SQ SIN SQ JKT312.00 NUC312.00 END ROE1.000000

The following are used in the fare calculation to indicate a connecting point, stopover charge, local surcharge, fare differential, or a surface segment.

| | |
|---|---|
| -X | Connecting city |
| S | Stopover charge |
| Q | Surcharge |
| D | Differential |
| /- | Surface segment |

As an example, consider the following fare calculation:

ATL DL SFO230.00Q7 /-SJC AA DFW260.00Q2 490.00 END

In this example, a surface segment exists between SFO and SJC.

**Inserting the Base Fare and Tax**

The secondary action code Y is used to insert the base fare and tax for each line, as follows:

W‡I‡Y<Base Fare>/<Tax>

**Example**:
W‡I‡Y420.38/33.62

Y is always input, regardless of the booking class or fare basis. The amounts must be entered with decimals or cents, without a dollar sign. The base fare and tax will be printed in the base fare and tax boxes on the ticket.

**Displaying a Ticket Record**

The fare information in a ticket record may be displayed as follows:

**W

When this entry is input, SABRE responds as follows:

```
T-ADT   0 CNT
1 O PDX AS   85Y 22SEP   705A OK
2 O ANC YC 143Y 26SEP   500P OK
    ENA
PDX AS ANC210.00Y YC ENA90.00Y 300.00 END
```

### Inserting Tour Codes

A ticket record for a tour itinerary must include the tour number and routing code. The qualifier RF is used to indicate that the routing is foreign. A tour number is entered with the secondary action code U.

W‡I‡U<Tour Number>‡R<Routing>

### Example:
W‡I‡UAMF3131‡RF

If a routing code is not inserted in the ticket record, SABRE will assume the routing is domestic.
Information may be inserted in a ticket record with one entry as follows:

W‡I‡L1-YXIT21‡L2-YWIT21*10MAY01JUN‡Y637.00/3.00‡KP5‡UAMF3113‡RF

This example will insert the line entitlement, validity dates, base fare and tax, commission, tour code, and routing indicator.

### Other Rate Desk Pricing Entries

The secondary code ED is used to input information in the ticket record to print in the endorsements/restrictions box on the ticket, as follows:

W‡EDSUBJ GVT APVL

This example would be used to indicate that the ticket is subject to government approval.
Multiple tax amounts may be input if more than one tax applies. Each tax should be identified by the two-letter country code, as follows:

W‡I‡Y290.00/29.00US/4.75CA

In this example, the U.S. tax is 29.00, and the Canadian tax is 4.75.
If a fare is tax exempt, the secondary code TE is inserted in place of the tax, as follows:

W‡I‡Y250.00/TE

In this example, the base fare is 250.00, but the fare is tax exempt. This entry might be used for special government travel for which U.S. transportation tax does not apply.

## Multiple Ticket Records

When passengers are to be ticketed using different passenger types, SABRE creates a separate ticket record for each passenger type (one for ADT, one for CHD). The following entries may be used with multiple ticket records.

| | |
|---|---|
| **W1 | Display first ticket record |
| **W2 | Display second ticket record |
| W‡CR1 | Re-create first ticket record |
| W‡CR2 | Re-create second ticket record |

## Ticket Issuance

The following format is used to issue tickets from a manual ticket record:

W‡T<Option>

The PNR must be ended and retrieved before tickets can be issued. To end transaction and print tickets with one entry, the following may be used:

EW‡T

An option, such as the form of payment or issuing carrier, may be included in the ticketing entry, as in the following example:

W‡T‡FINV‡AGA

This entry will print CK in the form-of-payment box on the ticket, and print Delta Airlines in the issuing airline box. If a carrier is not specified, the first carrier in the itinerary is used as the issuing airline.

The same form-of-payment formats that are used with demand ticketing may be used with

# Review

1. Write the entry to create a ticket record.

2. Write the entry to create a ticket record for segments 1 and 5 only.

3. Write the entry to create a ticket record to price the passengers using both adult and child fares.

4. What entry will insert the fare basis YLE3 for segments 1 and 5?

5. Write the entry to insert the fare basis YEE3M for segments 2 and 4.

6. What entry will insert the fare basis YLE for segment 1 and YLEE1M for segment 2?

7. Write the entry to insert a commission rate of 9 percent.

8. Write the entry to insert a commission of 23.80.

9. Write the entry to insert the fare calculation for the following itinerary:

```
1 BA   24Y 12MAR 3 SFOLHR HK1   145P  610A
2 BD  100Y 13MAR 4 LHRAMS HK1   900A 1000A
```

The fare from San Francisco to London is 942.00, and the fare from London to Amsterdam is 180.00. The fare basis is Y in both segments. The ROE is 1.000000.

10. Assume a PNR has the following itinerary:

```
1 WN 803Q 11JAN 3 SANABQ HK2   805A 1135A
2 WN 669Q 15JAN 7 ABQSAN HK2   310P  400P
```

What entry would be used to create a ticket record for the SANABQ segment?

11. Write the entry to redisplay the ticket record.

12. What entry would be used to insert the tour code AWA1924, indicating that the routing is foreign?

13. Write the entry to issue a ticket from a manual ticket record, indicating invoice as the form of payment and SQ as the issuing carrier.

# Electronic Miscellaneous Documents

## Objectives

*After completing this unit, you should be able to do the following:*

1. Input Air Extras by means of a fill-in mask.
2. Sell Air Extras from a list of available options/
3. Issue an EMD-S or an EMD-A.

## EMDs

An Electronic Miscellaneous Document (EMD) may be issued as payment for ancillary services such as baggage fees, change fees, lounge access, seat selection, and so forth. Two types of EMDs can be issued:

1. A Standalone EMD, or **EMD-S**, is issued for a non-flight related service, such as a change (rebooking) fee or group deposit.

2. An Associated EMD, or **EMD-A**, is issued for a flight related service, such as seat selection, pet transport, baggage fees, lounge access, etc.

Each EMD must contain two codes indicating the type of service: an RFIC (Reason For Issue Code), and an RFISC (Reason For Issue Sub-Code). The following are examples of RFIC categories:

| RFIC | Description | Examples |
|------|-------------|----------|
| A | Air transportation | Upgrades, charter fee |
| B | Non-air services | Shuttle, coach |
| C | Baggage fees | Checked or excess baggage |
| D | Financial impact | Change fee, deposit |
| E | Airport services | Check-in, lounge access |
| F | Merchandise | Apparel, coffee mugs |
| G | In-flight services | Beverage, blanket |
| H | Airline use only | (Varies by carrier) |

Within each RFIC category, separate sub-codes are used to indicate the specific service. The services that are available depend on the airline and are found on the carrier's EMD Fact Sheet. The following are examples:

| Service | RFIC | RFISC | EMD Type |
|---------|------|-------|----------|
| Seat selection | A | 0B5 | EMD-A |
| Ticket fee | D | 991 | EMD-S |
| Change fee - international | D | 993 | EMD-S |
| Change fee - domestic | D | 994 | EMD-S |
| Group deposit | D | 997 | EMD-S |
| Lounge access | E | 0BX | EMD-A |

| | | | |
|---|---|---|---|
| Second checked bag | C | 0CD | EMD-A |
| Third checked bag | C | 0CE | EMD-A |

The itinerary must be ticketed before an EMD-S may be issued.

## Entering an EMD-S

An Air Extras (AE) item must be entered in the PNR before an EMD-S can be issued. AE items are entered by means of a fill-in mask. The following entry will display the AE mask:

    AE‡EMD

*Response:*

```
PASSENGER NAME LINDBERG/CHARLES MR
TICKETING AIRLINE CODE< > SVC CITY<   > SVC DATE<     >
REASON FOR ISSUANCE CODE< > REASON FOR ISSUANCE SUBCODE<   >
TYPE OF SERVICE <                       > D/I < >
PRESENT TO <                 >
AT <                           >
BASE AMT <       > CURRENCY <   >
EQUIVALENT AMT PAID <     > <    > TAX EXEMPT < >
TAX/TAX CODE <      >< > < >< >
ENDORSEMENTS <                         >
PHONE CITY<   > PHN NBR<           > PHN TYPE< >
RECD FROM < >
CONNECTED TKT NUMBER<    >< > NEXT < > QUIT < >
```

The fields are defined as follows:

| | |
|---|---|
| TICKETING AIRLINE CODE | Applicable carrier code (2 characters) |
| SVC CITY | Departure city code (3 characters) |
| SVC DATE | Departure date (5 characters) |
| REASON FOR ISSUANCE CODE | RFIC (1 character) |
| REASON FOR ISSUANCE SUBCODE | RFICS (3 characters) |
| TYPE OF SERVICE | Text description |
| D/I | Domestic/International (1 character) |
| PRESENT TO | Airline or vendor name |
| AT | Airport or office name |
| BASE AMT | Fee amount |
| CURRENCY | Currency code (3 characters) |
| EQUIVALENT AMOUNT PAID | Amount paid in different currency |
| TAX EXEMPT | Type X to indicate (1 character) |
| TAX/TAX CODE | Tax amount/code (if applicable) |
| ENDORSEMENTS | Ticket endorsements or restrictions |
| PHONE CITY | Contact phone city code (3 characters) |
| PHN NBR | Contact phone |
| PHN TYPE | Contact phone type (1 character) |
| RECD FROM | Received from |
| CONNECTED TKT NUMBER | Ticket number issued in connection with |
| NEXT | Type X and Enter to input additional taxes |
| QUIT | Type X amd Enter to process the Air Extra |

138

If additional taxes apply, the agent types X in the NEXT field and then presses Enter. A second mask will be displayed with fields for multiple tax amounts and codes.

The following is an example of a completed AE mask:

```
PASSENGER NAME LINDBERG/CHARLES MR
TICKETING AIRLINE CODE<AA> SVC CITY<MIA> SVC DATE<18OCT>
REASON FOR ISSUANCE CODE<D> REASON FOR ISSUANCE SUBCODE<992>
TYPE OF SERVICE <CHANGE FEE              > D/I <I>
PRESENT TO <AMERICAN AIRLINES >
AT <MIAMI AIRPORT                   >
BASE AMT <100.00> CURRENCY <USD>
EQUIVALENT AMT PAID <      > <    > TAX EXEMPT < >
TAX/TAX CODE <      >< > < >< >
ENDORSEMENTS <NONREFUNDABLE                >
PHONE CITY<MIA> PHN NBR<305 558-1922> PHN TYPE<B>
RECD FROM <P>
CONNECTED TKT NUMBER<001><0872102986> NEXT < > QUIT <X>
```

## Displaying Air Extras

The following entry may be used to display the sold Air Extra(s) in a PNR:

> *AE

*Response:*

```
ANCILLARY SERVICES
  1.CHANGE FEE      1.1 LINDBERG/CHARLES MR
    STATUS - HN1/REQUESTED
    AMOUNT - 75.00EUR
    TOTAL  - 75.00EUR
    DOC/CF - 1250819762022 CPN -01
```

In this example, the status code HN indicates that the Air Extra has been requested. When the service is confirmed by the airline, the status will be changed to HD.

## Selling an EMD-A

An EMD-A can be sold from a list of available Air Extras. The following entry will display the available Air Extras for a booked itinerary:

> WPAE

*Response:*

```
AIR EXTRAS
BG-BAGGAGE                          CXR  SEG/CPA        FEE
1   ADT-CHECKED BAG FIRST            SA  1-JNBCPT   350.00 N
2   ADT-CHECKED BAG SECOND           SA  1-JNBCPT   350.00 N
3   ADT-CHECKED BAG THIRD            SA  1-JNBCPT   350.00 N

N SERVICE IS NONREFUNDABLE
/ FEE APPLIES FOR EACH SELECTED ITEM
```

The following entry is used to sell a selected service:

AE‡1A1

This entry will sell the service in line 1 of the Air Extras list.

## Issuing an EMD

Before an EMD can be issued, the status of the AE item must be HD, indicating that the Air Extra has been confirmed by the airline. The following entry is used to issue the EMD:

W‡EMD*AE1

This entry will issue the EMD for AE item 1 in the PNR.

### Optional Qualifiers

| | |
|---|---|
| Form of payment | W‡EMD*AE1‡F*AX330517289930990/1218 |
| Validating carrier | W‡EMD*AE1-5‡BA |
| Commission | W‡EMD*AE1‡KP5 |
| Name selection | W‡EMD*AE1‡N1.2 |

## Review

1. What entry is used to display an Air Extras mask for issuing an EMD-S?

2. What entry will display the available Air Extras for a booked itinerary?

3. What entry would be used to sell Air Extra item 3?

4. What entry would be used to display the sold Air Extras in a PNR?

5. What entry will issue the EMD for Air Extras item 1?

# Glossary

**A**

**address field**  A part of a PNR for storing address information. A PNR may have two address fields: one for a client address and another for the agency address.

**advance purchase**  A fare rule requiring the ticket to be purchased a preset number of days prior to departure.

**air itinerary**  An itinerary containing only flight segments; the flight segments of an itinerary that also contains auxiliary segments.

**airline code**  An alpha or numeric code assigned to each airline by IATA. The alpha airline code, also called the carrier code, consists of two or three letters, whereas the numeric code consists of three digits.

**airport code**  A three-letter code assigned to each airport by IATA.

**air segment**  The representation of an airline flight in an itinerary. Also called a flight segment.

**alpha**  Consisting only of letters.

**alphanumerical**  Consisting of a combination of numbers, letters, or punctuation.

**American plan**  (AP)  A hotel rate that includes lodging and two or three daily meals. Also called full pension.

**AP**  In a fare display, an abbreviation for advance purchase; in hotel reservations, an abbreviation for American Plan.

**ARINC**  An independent data communications network that links computer reservation systems with airlines.

**arrival point**  The second city or airport code in a city pair. Also called the off point or destination.

**ARNK**  Abbreviation for "arrival unknown," the representation of a surface segment in an air itinerary to maintain continuity between flight segments.

**AT**  (global indicator) travel via the Atlantic.

**ATB stock**  Ticket forms for issuing an auto-mated ticket and boarding pass (ATB).

**autoprice**  To use a CRS to fare an itinerary automatically.

**auxiliary segment**  Any segment of an itinerary other than an air segment.

**availability**  A display of regularly scheduled flights between a specified origin and destination. Also, a display of room types or car types available during a specified period.

## B

**bedding code**  A code that indicates the number and size of beds provided at a specific room rate.

**base fare**  The fare excluding tax.

**Best Buy**  The entry to fare an itinerary at the lowest available fare regardless of the classes in which the segments are booked.

**board point**  Any point where a passenger boards an aircraft; the first point in a city pair or air segment. Also called a departure point or origin point.

**book**  To arrange a reservation for transportation or accommodations; to sell a travel product or service.

**booking agent**  A person or business that books reservations on behalf of a travel vendor; the travel agent responsible for a specific reservation.

**booking class**  The code for the class of service, used to obtain a selected fare basis when an air segment is sold. Also called the booking code or booking class code.

**booking source**  The travel agency or other seller that is responsible for a reservation.

**business class**  A class of service on an airline flight, priced higher than standard coach class but lower than first class.

## C

**cabin**  A passenger compartment on an airline flight. The standard cabins are first class, business class, and economy (also called coach, standard, or middle class).

**cancel**  To remove a segment from an itinerary and return the space to the vendor's inventory.

**car**  Any type of rental vehicle offered by an automobile and truck rental firm.

**car availability**  A display of vendors and car types for a specified city and date.

**car company**  Any vendor that rents vehicles on a daily basis.

**car type availability**  A car availability display that does not include rate information.

**car type code**  A code identifying the vehicle class, body type, type of shift, and air conditioning.

**carrier**  A company that provides transportation service.

**central processor**  In a data processing system, the component that processes data and coordinates the communication, storage, and retrieval of data.

**child fare**  A discount fare for a child under a specified age.

**circle trip**  An itinerary in which the passenger returns to the origin point.

**city code**  A three-letter code designated by the International Standards Organization for a city served by passenger air carriers.

**city pair**  A six-letter code consisting of city or airport codes for a board point and an off point.

**claim a reservation**  To retrieve a booking created by another booking source for ticketing.

**class**  A designation of the level of service and price on an airline flight.

**client profile**  A computer record that contains passenger data items for a frequent traveler.

**coach**  The standard class of service offered by an airline; any large passenger vehicle operated for intra-city bus service or sight-seeing excursions.

**combinability**  A fare rule that states whether a specific booking code or fare basis can be combined with other booking codes or fare bass. Also called a combination rule.

**commission**  A percentage of the sale price of a product, paid by a vendor to a third-party seller.

**commuter carrier**  An airline that operates small aircraft and provides service within a limited geographic area.

**computer reservation system**  (CRS) A computer system designed for use by booking agents to facilitate the sale of travel products and services of participating vendors.

**configuration**  The interior arrangement of an aircraft or other transportation vehicle.

**connecting point**  A city or airport where a passenger must change from one flight to another.

**connection**  Air transportation requiring a transfer from one flight to another.

**corporate rate**  A discounted hotel rate offered to business travelers. A discounted car rental rate that has been negotiated with a company.

**CRS**  Abbreviation for computer reservation system.

# D

**data**  Information that can be processed by a computer.

**data communications**  The process of transmitting and receiving computer data.

**data field**  The part of a record in which a data item is stored.

**data item**  An item of information, such as a name, telephone number, or remark, stored in a PNR field.

**days of operation**  Days of the week on which a flight operates; also called frequency of operation.

**day/time restriction**  A fare rule requiring departure on specified days of the week and/or at specified times of the day.

**decode**  To determine the name or word represented by a code such as a city, carrier, equipment, or vendor code.

**departure point**  The first point in a city pair;  any point from which a traveler departs. Also called the board point.

**deplane**  To disembark from an airplane.

**destination**  A traveler's intended arrival point; the last stopping point of an itinerary; the point of an itinerary to which the highest one-way full coach fare applies.

**destination point**  The second city or airport code in a city pair or air segment. Also called the arrival point.

**diabetic meal**  A meal that is fit to be eaten by a person who has diabetes, in conformance with medical instructions or guidelines.

**direct-access availability**  A flight availability display obtained by linking with an airline's reservation system.

**direct flight**  A flight that does not involve a change of flight number.

**direct-sell**  To book an airline reservation by typing the carrier code, flight number, class, date, city pair, action code, and number of seats.

**disembark**  To leave an aircraft or ship.

**domestic**  Within or belonging to a particular country.

**domestic fare**  A fare that applies to travel between points within the specific country in which the travel agency is located. Also, any fare for a domestic flight.

**domestic flight**  A flight that both departs and arrives within the boundaries of the specific country in which the travel agency is based.

**double bed**  A bed with a standard mattress designed to accommodate two people. Also called a French bed.

**double occupancy**  A hotel room that is occupied by two adults.

**double rate**  A hotel rate for a room that will be occupied by two adults.

**downline space**  Any segment of an itinerary after the originating flight.

**E**

**economy class**  An airline's standard level of service for travel in the coach cabin.

**EH**  (global indicator) Eastern Hemisphere

**elapsed flight time**  The total elapsed time of an airline flight from departure to arrival.

**EM**  (global indicator) Travel via Europe and the Middle East.

**encode**  To determine the code for a name or word such as a city, airline, aircraft equipment, or hotel chain.

**end transact**  End the transaction.

**end the transaction**  To transmit an assembled PNR to the central processor for permanent storage.

**endorsement**  On an airline ticket, written authorization from an airline permitting the passenger to travel on a different carrier.

**endorsement/restrictions box**  The part of an airline ticket where endorsements or restrictions are printed.

**equipment**  In aviation, the type of aircraft used for transport.

**equipment code**  A three-letter code designating the type of aircraft used for a passenger flight or cargo transport.

**EP**  Abbreviation for European plan.

**escorted tour**  A package tour that includes the services of a tour escort.

**ETA**  Abbreviation for estimated time of arrival.

**ETD**  Abbreviation for estimated time of departure.

**e-ticket**  Electronic ticket, also called a paperless ticket.

**European plan**  A hotel rate that includes accommodations only, without meals.

**exception**  Days of the week on which a flight does not operate; also called frequency exception.

**exchange**  In ticketing, the issuance of a new ticket to replace a ticket that was issued previously, as a result of an itinerary change.

**excursion**  A short journey that returns to its starting point.

**excursion fare**  A round-trip fare that is less expensive than the combined cost of the component one-way fares.

**F**

**family plan**  In the lodging industry, a policy permitting children of a specified age to stay free of charge in the same room as their parents; in the transportation industry, a discount plan offered to members of a family travelling together.

**fare**  The fee paid by a traveler for transport on an airline, bus, or train.

**fare basis**  A preset price level for air travel, designated by a code and defined by a combination of travel restrictions.

**fare calculation**  A delineation of the total fare for an itinerary by board point, carrier, and off point, based on the fare basis of each segment.

**fare construction**  The calculation of international fares based on IATA guidelines and based on Neutral Units of Construction (NUC).

**fare display**  A display of fares between a specified origin and destination. Also called a fare quote or tariff display.

**fare rule**  A description of the booking code, validity or ticketing dates, and any restrictions that apply to a particular fare basis.

**field identifier**  A code that indicates the field where information is to be stored.

**first class**  The premium class of service and highest fare offered by an airline; also called premium class.

**flight**  A regularly scheduled air transport service.

**flight number**  A number consisting of one to four digits assigned to each flight.

**flight segment**  The portion of an itinerary representing a reservation to travel on an airline flight.

**form of payment**  An abbreviation or other text indicating the method by which airline tickets will be purchase, such as cash, a bank check, or a credit card.

**form of payment box**  The part of an airline ticket where the form of payment is printed.

**frequency**  Days of the week on which a flight operates.

**frequency exception**  Days of the week on which a flight does not operate.

**G**

**global indicator**  A two-letter code identifying the applicable global routing direction for a fare.

**government travel request**  (GTR) A document issued by a government agency authorizing a travel agency or airline to issue a ticket.

**group rate**  A hotel rate offered to members of a group such as a trade association, corporation, or fraternal organization, based on a guarantee to occupy a minimum number of rooms.

**guarantee**  A promise to pay for a hotel reservation whether or not it is fulfilled. Common methods of guaranteeing a reservation include a deposit, credit card number, or corporate address.

**guaranteed flight segment**  A flight segment that was booked by linking with the carrier's reservation system.

**H**

**high season**  A period of high demand; also called a peak period.

**hotel availability**  A display listing hotels and rate categories that are available during a specified date range.

**hotel description**  A detailed record containing about facilities, credit card policies, family plan, and other information about a specific property.

**hotel index**  A list of hotels that are located in a specified city and permit reservations to be booked through the CRS.
I

**IATA**  International Air Transport Association.

**ignore**  To remove a PNR from the work area without transmitting the record to the central processor for permanent storage.

**in-flight service**  Entertainment meals, beverages, or miscellaneous items provided during a flight.

**in-plant**  a department or division of a company set up to handle the travel requirements of the company or its employees.

**input**  To enter data to a computer for processing.

**inter-line**  Between different carriers. An inter-line connection involves flights operated by different carriers.

**in-terminal**  Located in an airport terminal.  Also called on-premises.

**international airline**  Any airline that provides service to or from a foreign point; an airline that is based in a country other than the one where the travel agency is located.

**International Air Transport Association**  (IATA) A voluntary organization of international airlines established to coordinate airfares, establish service standards, and provide a unified system of worldwide air transportation.

**issuing carrier**  The airline that authorizes a ticket to be issued by a retail travel agency and certifies that the ticket is valid for carriage over the designated routing. Also called the validating carrier.

**itinerary**  A list of points, routes, and transportation carriers for a trip.

**itinerary/invoice**  A document that provides detailed flight information for each segment and a summary of all the charges.

**J**

**joint fare**  A fare using two or more carriers via a specified  routing.

**K**

**keyword**  A code consisting of three or more alpha characters that can be used to retrieve information from storage or to select an item from a menu.

**king bed**  A bed with the largest mattress size designed to accommodate two people.

**kosher meal**  A meal that is fit to be eaten in conformance with Jewish dietary and ceremonial laws.

**L**

**lacto-ovo vegetarian meal**  A meal that is prepared only from vegetables, milk, and eggs.

**layover**  A time interval between points in an itinerary; actual connecting time.

**leg**  A segment of a connection or, if a direct flight involves a change of aircraft, any portion between a board point and an off point.

**local fare**  A fare published in the currency of a specified country for air travel originating in that country.

**local time**  The time in a specified location.

**location indicator**  A code in a phone entry designating whether the telephone number is for a travel agency, client business, or home.

**low-to-high display**  A display of fares or rates listed from least expensive to most expensive.

**low season**  A period of low demand; also called an off-peak period.

**M**

**mainframe**  Computer hardware consisting of a powerful central processor and a large storage area.

**MAP**  Abbreviation for modified American plan.

**market**  The geographical area served by a specific flight, hotel, or car rental outlet.

**maximum permitted mileage** (MPM) In international fare construction, the maximum number of miles permitted between two points to obtain a designated point-to-point fare.

**MCO**  Miscellaneous Charges Order.

**menu**  A list of options that can be selected by an item number or keyword.

**meal plan**  A hotel rate that includes one or more daily meals.

**mileage system**  A method of calculating international fares based on the maximum permitted mileage between two points.

**military passenger**  A traveler who qualifies for a discount military fare.

**minimum connecting time**  The minimum time permitted between connecting flights.

**Miscellaneous Charges Order**  (MCO) A document issued by a travel agency or vendor authorizing a travel service for a specified individual.

**modem**  (modulator/demodulator) A device that converts computer data into signals that can be transmitted over a telephone line.

**modified American plan** (MAP) A hotel rate that includes accommodations and two meals, usually breakfast and dinner.

**MPM** Abbreviation for maximum permitted mileage.

**N**

**name field** The part of a PNR in which a passenger's name is stored.

**Neutral Unit of Construction** (NUC) A standard monetary unit used to calculate international fares, adjusted to international currency rates.

**nonstop** A direct flight that does not stop between the origin point and the passenger's intended destination.

**NUC** Abbreviation for Neutral Unit of Construction.

**numerical** Consisting only of numbers.

**O**

**off-line** Services provided by a carrier other than the ticketing airline. Any airline other than the host carrier.

**off point** The second point in a city pair; any point at which a passenger disembarks.

**off-premises** Not located on the premises of an airport.

**on-line connection** A connection requiring a change of flights operated by the same airline.

**one-way** An itinerary in which the traveler will not return to the originating point.

**on-premises** Located on the premises of an airport (see in-terminal).

**onward segment** The next flight segment after a specific segment.

**open jaw** A circle trip with a surface portion at the outward destination or just before the return segment to the originating point.

**open segment** A reservation to travel on a specific carrier without a specified flight number.

**operator** In mathematics, a symbol used to designate an arithmetic operation such as multiplication or division.

**origin** Any point from which a traveler departs; the first departure point in an itinerary.

**originating carrier** The first carrier in an air itinerary.

**originating point** The first point of departure in an itinerary.

**OSI** (optional service information or other service information) A message that is input to a CRS to advise an airline about some aspect of a reservation, such as a child's age, an elderly passenger, or a VIP.

**outbound segment** The first segment in an air itinerary; the segment that departs from the originating point.

**output** To generate data from a computer for display, hard copy, or storage.

**overbook** To intentionally book more reservations than the capacity of the flight or hotel, to compensate for no-shows and cancellations.

**P**

**PA** (global indicator) travel via the Pacific

**passenger** A person who travels on a transportation carrier.

**passenger facility charge** (PFC) A surcharge imposed by an airport for construction or improvements.

**passenger type code** A code used, for pricing purposes, to indicate whether a passenger is an adult, a child, a discount group passenger, etc.

**passive segment** A segment representing air space booked directly with a carrier by a means other than the CRS.

**peak period** A period of high demand; also called a high season.

**PFC** Abbreviation for passenger facility charge.

**PNR** Abbreviation for passenger name record. A computer record containing the itinerary, passenger names, contact telephone numbers, ticketing arrangement, and other data relating to a reservation.

**Prepaid Ticket Advice** (PTA) An authorization to issue a ticket at a location other than the point of purchase.

**prereserved seat** A seat assignment that is made prior to check-in.

**promotional fare** A reduced fare offered by a carrier during a special promotion or to encourage sales during a period of low demand.

**promotional rate** A special room rate offered by a hotel in conjunction with an advertising campaign. A car rental rate that has specific restrictions, such as an advance reservation requirement or a minimum rental period.

**pseudocity** A code that identifies each site where CRS terminals are installed. Also called a branch code.

## Q

**qualified availability** A display of car availability and rates by vendor and car type.

**queen bed** A bed with a mattress larger than a double bed but smaller than a king bed.

**queue** An electronic holding area for messages or passenger records awaiting special attention by an agent.

**quota** A preset quantity of a product or service; the maximum number of airline seats that may be sold in one transaction with immediate confirmation.

**quote** To communicate a fare or rate to a prospective client; a fare quotation.

## R

**rack rates** The normal room rates offered by a hotel to the general public.

**rate category** Special hotel or car rental rates, such as association, corporate, promotional, and convention rates.

**rate plan** The basis for a car rental rate, such as daily, weekly, monthly, and weekend rates.

**rate quote** A display of available car types and rates in a specific market.

**rate type** The price level for a room rate, such as rack, corporate, promotional, and group rates.

**reconfirm** To state an intention to fulfill a reservation.

**received-from field** A part of a PNR in which text is stored to indicate the source of the reservation.

**record** A collection of related data, such as a passenger reservation.

**record locator** A six-character code displayed when a transaction is ended, and by which the PNR can be retrieved from storage.

**reference-sell** To sell a segment by line number from an availability display.

**remarks field** A part of a PNR in which free-form text is stored to communicate information to other agents in the office, or to remind the agent to take some future action.

**reservation**  An arrangement to occupy an accommodation on a transportation carrier or in a lodging establishment.

**restricted fare**  A discounted coach fare subject to restrictions.

**restriction**  A condition, such as advance purchase or a minimum stay, for travel at a specific fare basis.

**return availability**  A display of flights for the opposite city pair of the previous availability display.

**return segment**  In a circle trip, the segment that arrives at the originating point.

**room option**  An optional request input with a hotel reservation, such as a charge for an extra guest, an adult or child rollaway, or a crib.

**room rate**  The charge for a specific room type based on the rate type and category.

**room type**  A code consisting of the room category and bedding offered for a specific room rate.

**round trip**  A circle trip with one stopover; a journey consisting of direct transportation from one point to another, returning to the point of origin.

**round-trip fare**  A fare that requires round-trip travel on the same carrier and/or in an equivalent class of service on all segments.

**round-trip indicator**  A code in a fare display designating a round-trip fare.

**route**  To arrange or specify connecting points.

**routing**  The permitted connecting and stopping points for a particular fare.

**rule**  Fare restriction.

**S**

**screen**  Video display terminal; an information display.

**scroll**  To move text vertically on the screen to search for specific information.

**seat assignment**  A record of the row and seat to be occupied by a passenger on a specific flight segment.

**seat map**  A display showing the status of all the seats on a specific flight.

**seat quota**  On a specific airline flight, the number of seats that can be sold in each class of service in one transaction, based on the carrier's agreement with Sabre.

**sector**  In fare calculation, a specific flight segment or a specific segment of a connection. segment  A specific portion of an itinerary, such as an airline flight or hotel reservation; in an air itinerary, any point-to-point flight reservation.

**segment status**  A two-letter code indicating the status of a reservation. For example, HK indicates a confirmed reservation, and HL indicates a waitlisted reservation that has not yet been confirmed.

**senior**  An elderly passenger.

**sign in**  To input an entry to identify the agent and gain access to the CRS.

**sign out**  To input an entry to exit from the CRS.

**similar name list**  A display of the names and departure dates of PNRs that have the same or similar names.

**sine**  Sign-on code.

**single occupancy**  A hotel rate based on a room occupied by one adult.

**single supplement**  A surcharge assessed to a client who will travel unaccompanied but purchases a product that is priced on the basis of double occupancy.

**Standard Interline Passenger Procedures**  (SIPP) A standard coding system for the CRS industry, enabling airline reservation systems to exchange data with other vendors.

**space**  A reservation to travel on a transportation carrier or to occupy a hotel room.

**special meal**  A meal ordered on an airline flight, other than one normally served to passengers.

**SSR**  (special service requirement or request) Special service or assistance not normally provided to passengers, such as a wheelchair or special meal. Also called a special service request.

**stand-by**  Travel offered or arranged without a confirmed reservation, based on available space at the time of departure.

**stand-by fare**  A reduced fare for stand-by travel.

**stopover**  Any point in an itinerary that is not a connecting point; a point where the interval exceeds 4 hours between domestic flights or 12 hours between international flights.

**surcharge**  A charge added to a basic fare for airport improvements or security, travel during a peak period, or other reasons.

**surface segment**  A segment in which the passenger will travel by a means other than air transportation.

# T

**tariff**  Fare information for transportation carriers; any schedule of airfares.

**terminal**  Airport facilities used by an airline. Also, a computer workstation consisting of a keyboard and a video display screen.

**throughfare**  A fare covering all legs of a connection and less than the combined fares of each leg if priced separately.

**ticket**  A document that entitles the bearer to passage on a transportation carrier.

**ticketing field**  A part of a PNR in which ticketing details are stored. Also called the ticketing arrangement field.

**time limit**  An arrangement by which tickets must be purchased by a preset date and time to avoid automatic cancellation of the itinerary.

**title**  An abbreviation such as MR, MRS, MISS, or MSTR, used in a name entry to clarify the sex, age group, and marital or occupational status of each traveler.

**tour**  A package trip consisting of two or more components such as airfare, accommodations, a car rental, or other services; any travel product offered for resale by a tour wholesaler.

**tour basis**  A reduced fare for a passenger who purchase a prepaid tour.

**tour number**  A code identifying a specific travel product offered for resale by a tour vendor.

**travel agency**  A retail business authorized to sell travel products on behalf of vendors such as airlines, ships, rail companies, and lodging establishments.

**TS**  (global indicator) Trans-Siberian routing.

**twin bed**  A bed with a mattress designed for one person.

# U

**unaccompanied minor**  A child 11 years or younger traveling without an adult.

# V

**validity dates**  The dates between which a special fare or hotel rate is valid.

**validate**  To imprint an airline or rail ticket with the trademark and airline code of the issuing carrier and the name, address, and IATA identification code of the issuing agency.

**validating carrier**  The airline that issued the validation plates that are used to validate a ticket; also called the issuing carrier.

**validation**  Authorization by an airline that a ticket is valid for carriage on the designated airline(s) and routing.

**vegetarian meal**  A meal that does not contain any meat or dairy products.

**vendor**  The provider of a product or service offered for sale through a CRS.

**VIP**  A very important passenger such as a high-ranking airline executive, diplomat, or government representative.

# W

**waitlist**  A list of passengers who desire a confirmed reservation for accommodations that were sold out at the time the reservation was requested; to place a reservation on such a list.

**WH**  (global indicator) Western Hemisphere

**work area**  An electronic holding area in which  passenger data items are assembled before  they are transmitted to the central processor .

# Answers to Review Questions

## Introduction

1. SIA15432
2. SO*
3. W/-ALALITALIA
4. W/*CX
5. W/*KHI
6. W/-CCSEOUL
7. W/-APGATWICK
8. W/EQ-FOKKER
9. WEQ*M80
10. W/-ALLUFTHANSA

## Availability

1. 119MARCLERDU1P
2. 1*
3. 1*3P
4. 116JUL11A
5. 124MAYMSPAMS2P/D
6. 130APRSYDLAX–C
7. 112FEBMIACPT‡SA
8. 1R27FEB6P
9. 118MAYATLSEA8ADEN
10. 1AA331Y18OCTDFWLAX

## Selling Air Segments

1. b
2. (a) Y
   (b) 3
   (c) 2
3. (a) 04Y3
   (b) 02K4
   (c) 01H5
4. (a) Y
   (b) 3
   (c) Wednesday
   (d) MEL
   (e) 655A (on Thursday)
5. 01C3*
6. 03C5Y6
7. 0BA510C13DECLAXLHRNN1
8. 0UA189Y22MAYORDSFOLL1
9. ARNK

10. 0A
11. 0PI14S20JULNANSVUGK2
12. 0UAOPENCFRAIADDS1

## Passenger Name Records

1. –
2. –MOORE/THOMAS MR
3. –2CLEMSON/ALAN MR/JANE MRS
4. –4LIONEL/WARREN MR/MARY MRS/J MSTR/E MISS
5. –4STEGLITZ/FRANZ MR/BEATRICE MRS/G MR/H MISS
6. 9
7. 9415-753-4332-A
8. 9305-640-2872-H
9. 9404-664-0987-B
10. 7
11. 7TAW19JUL/
12. 6
13. 6P
14. 6MR POUNDSTONE

## Supplementary Data

1. Remarks
2. 5
3. 5MAIL TICKETS
4. 5-CK
5. 5-*AX3650513240402212‡10/18
6. 5-CASH
7. 3
8. YY
9. 3OSI BA VIP JAPANESE CONSUL
10. 4OSI ELDERLY PSGR
11. UNMR
    DEAF
    BLND
    WCHR
    WCHS
    WCHC
    VGML
    KSML
12. 3BLND
13. 3VGML–2.1
14. W–TICKET EXPRESS‡8254 CACTUS BLVD‡PHOENIX AZ 85023
15. 5/MR T MATHEWSΣ5/52 OAK STΣ5/FT LAUDERDALE FL 33329
16. PE‡HCHUNG@GEOSYS.NET‡FR/AGENT NAME
17. EM
18. 3DOCS/P/US/60755484/US/28APR65/F/12JAN20/LARSEN/KRISTIN-1.1
19. 3DOCO/MIAMI/V/877365507/MIAMI/12NOV14/CN-1.1

## Modifying the Itinerary

1. *-TEMPLETON
2. *-GREENE
3. *-NORMAN
4. *AA2784/18JUN–KLEINMAN
5. *SWKLQH
6. *A
7. *I
8. *P
9. X
10. X3
11. X1
12. X1‡0015JUN
13. X1/3/7
14. XI
15. .4HK

## Modifying the PNR

1. ,
2. ,1
3. ,2
4. –2¤
5. ,1
6. D
7. F
8. D2
9. 3OSI BA TCP2 W/THOMAS BA742M18JUNLHRHKG
10. D1.1*2.1

## Fare Quotes

1. FQPARDEN17AUG
2. FQLONATH23MAR-OA
3. FQLONHKG28JAN‡RT-BA
4. FQ*19JUN
5. FQ*-DL
6. FQL4
7. FQLAXPER24MAR‡R2APR
8. RD2
9. RD6*M
10. RD*6
11. RDDENSEA31JULHLE21N-UA

## Itinerary Pricing

1. WP
2. WPS1/3/5
3. WPX5
4. WPNC
5. WPNCB
6. WPS4
7. (a) WPN1.2
   (b) WPP2ADT/CHD
8. PQ
9. WPRQ
10. *PQ

## Ticket Issuance

1. W‡
2. W‡AUA‡KP0‡FCK
3. W‡AAA‡KP0‡FCASH‡N2.2
4. W‡AMH‡KP2‡FCHECK
5. W‡ACO‡KP0‡FAX3003242498761234/0918
6. W‡AAA‡KP0‡FCASH‡EDNO REFUND
7. W‡ADL‡KP0‡FCHECK‡XETR

## Prereserved Seats

1. 4GA/A
2. 4G1/W
3. 4GA/SA
4. 4G3/23A
5. 4G2/14DEF
6. 4G*2
7. 4G*AA305Y21MARLHRJFK
8. *B
9. 4GX3/14C
10. 4G2,4/A

## Queues

1. queue 3
2. queue 9
3. QC/
4. Q/
5. the first PNR on queue
6. QE
7. QC/BW3R17
8. QU
9. QI
10. QX

11. QC/
12. QC/18
13. Q/18
14. QP/35/11

## Client Profiles

1. N*
2. NLIST/B
3. N*UNISYS
4. N*PACTEL–HARMAN
5. A
6. O
7. N
8. Special Traveler's Account Record
9. NM
10. NM7Σ9Σ11

## Hotel Reservations

1. HOTNCE
2. HOTNBO/HL
3. HOTMAD/A
4. HOT1/3NT1
5. HOTFRA/12JUN–17JUN2
6. HOD*3
7. 0H1‡2/G334659870917863EXP 07 18-DAVIS
8. 0H1‡3
9. 0H1‡5/RC–1
10. HOM2R/1A2Q–2
11. HOM3O/CR–1
12. HODIC
13. HCCC/ES*P

## Car Rentals

1. CQ5/6ZE
2. CF2/3
3. CFVIE/21AUG–25AUG/0900–1000/EC
4. CQ1/2/ZI/IC
5. CF*R2
6. CPZDLGW
7. 0C3
8. 0C6/ID–702635
9. CM5/CT–ECMR
10. CM3/PD–17JUN

## Miscellaneous Functions

1. V*BA42/12MAY  or  2BA42/12MAY
2. VA*4
3. VI*3
4. T*CT–CDG
5. T¤12MAY–28
6. DC*JPY  or  DC*JAPAN
7. DC‡NZD1750/CAD
8. T*JNB

## Phase IV Ticketing

1. W‡C
2. W‡C‡S1/5
3. W‡C‡PADT/CHD
4. W‡I‡L1/5-YLE3
5. W‡I‡L2/4-YEE3M
6. W‡I‡L1-YLE‡L2-YLEE1M
7. W‡I‡KP9
8. W‡I‡K23.80
9. W‡I‡CSFO BA LON942.00 BD AMS180.00 NUC1122.00 ROE1.000000
10. W‡C‡S2
11. **W
12. W‡I‡UAWA1924‡RF
13. W‡T‡FINV‡ASQ

## Electronic Miscellaneous Documents

1. AE‡EMD
2. WPAE
3. AE‡1A3
4. *AE
5. W‡EMD*AE1

# MUNDUS

To obtain the software to accompany this textbook, please contact|:

Admin@e-Mundus.com

Made in the USA
San Bernardino, CA
30 December 2018